Revise Modern World History
for Edexcel Specification A

Barry Doherty

Heinemann

Heinemann Educational Publishers
Halley Court, Jordan Hill, Oxford OX2 8EJ
Part of Harcourt Education
Heinemann is a registered trademark of Reed Educational &
Professional Publishing Ltd

First published 2001

ISBN 0 435 31145 X

04
10 9 8 7 6 5 4 3

Designed, illustrated and typeset by Techset Ltd, Gateshead

Printed and bound in UK by CPI Bath

Photographic acknowledgements
The author and publisher would like to thank the following for permission to
reproduce photographs:
Associated Press: 133 (top); Associated Press / Stringer: 89 (centre right);
Bildarchiv Preussischer Kulturbesitz: 50; Corbis: 89 (left, centre left, centre and
right); 112 (left, centre left and right); 133 (centre and bottom); David King:
27; Imperial War Museum: 15; Peter Newark's American Pictures: 38; 62;
Popperfoto: 112 (centre and centre right).

Cover photograph: © Imperial War Museum

Written source acknowledgements
The author and publisher gratefully acknowledge the following publications from
which written sources in the book are drawn. In some sentences the wording or
sentence structure may have been simplified:
E M Remarque, *All Quiet on the Western Front* (Jonathan Cape, 1984). Reprinted
by permission of The Random House Group Ltd: p.15;
John Steinbeck, *Of Mice and Men* (Penguin Books, 1949), copyright © John
Steinbeck, 1937. Reproduced by permission of Penguin Books Ltd: p.38

Dedication: for Tracy, my best friend and inspiration.

Contents

2, 3, 4, 8, 10, 11

Introduction

What do I study in Modern World History for Edexcel?

The Modern World History for GCSE course is one of three History courses studied at GCSE. (The others are Schools History Project and Aspects of Modern Social, Economic and Political History.)

Here is a summary of what you will be expected to study for the Modern World History specification:

Edexcel

Paper 1: 2 hours
Questions on Outline Studies:
The Road to War, 1870-1914;
Nationalism and Independence in India, c.1900-49;
The Emergence of Modern China, 1911-76;
The Rise and Fall of the Communist State: The Soviet Union, 1928-91;
A Divided Union? The USA, 1941-80;
Superpower Relations, 1945-90;
Conflict and the Quest for Peace in the Middle East, 1948-95.

You will be expected to know two of these Outline Studies and to answer one question on each. Questions will ask you to show your understanding of a number of key concepts, such as change over time, historical knowledge, and analysis of key features and events.

Paper 2: 1 hour 45 minutes
Questions on Depth Studies:
The Russian Revolution, c. 1910-24;
The War to End Wars, 1914-19;
Depression and the New Deal: the USA 1929-41;
Nazi Germany, c.1930-9;
The World at War, 1938-45;
The End of Apartheid in South Africa, 1982-94;
Conflict in Vietnam, c. 1963-75.

You will be expected to answer two questions on separate Depth Studies. The questions will test your ability to understand, analyse and evaluate a range of historical sources.

Coursework

You can do coursework on a programme of study related to the syllabus, but not on things you are going to answer questions on in the exam. You will be expected to complete two coursework assignments.

In each section you will find:

Topic summary

Sometimes studying history in depth can be confusing because you get to know so much detail that you lose sight of the 'big picture'. So we start each section with a summary of what the topic is about.

What do I need to know?

The revision guide then gives you a summary of what you need to know for the exam. Summary boxes are also included to give you a handy visual summary. When you have completed your revision you should be able to take a summary box and write at length about each point that is shown in it.

History of the topic

Here we give you the basic facts about the topic, but not in the same detail as in your textbook and notes. We are not telling you the whole story again, but instead are summarising it to make it easier for you to learn.

What do I know?

Once you have completed your revision you might like to test yourself to see how much you know. We have included short self-assessment sections so that you can see just how thorough your revision has been. Most of the questions can be answered from information given in the summary, but we also presume that you have been learning the information in your book and notes!

Exam type question

You may be studying history because you love it and not care about how you do in the exam. For most students, however, what they really want is to do as well as possible in the examination. So we have given you lots of examples of the types of questions you will be asked, together with some student answers.

Examiner's comments

The author of this book is an experienced teacher for this syllabus and he has commented on each exam question answer. By reading his comments you will be able to see what is good and what is disappointing in each answer. Then you can make sure that any answer you give in the exam is much better.

1. The war to end all wars, 1914–19

Topic Summary

Around 9 million people died during the First World War. A 300-year-old monarchy crumbled, civil wars broke out, civilians were faced with air raids and starvation, whilst soldiers endured horrors on a scale never seen before. Most expected the war to be 'over by Christmas', but the use of new technology and a determination on both sides to win the war created a bloody and prolonged stalemate. By 1918 all sides were exhausted by war and crippled with debts that left them with a decade of hardship after the war. The 1914-18 war was meant to be 'the war to end all wars', but the harshness of the Treaty of Versailles in 1919 meant that a second world war became more likely.

What do I Need to Know?

You will need to know why the First World War dragged on longer than most people predicted. You will also need to be aware of the conditions in which soldiers fought in the trenches, at sea and in the air. In addition you will need to understand why the war finally came to an end by 1918 and be able to discuss the punishment Germany received at the Versailles Conference.

Key Events

1 August 1914
Outbreak of the First World War.

5-10 September 1914
First Battle of the Marne.

10 September–18 October 1914
'Race for the Seas'.

February 1915–January 1916
Gallipoli Campaign.

22 April 1915
Gas first used on the Western Front, by the German army.

7 May 1915
Sinking of the *Lusitania* by a German U-boat.

21 February–18 December 1916
Battle of Verdun.

31 May–1 June 1916
Battle of Jutland.

1 June–19 November 1916
Battle of the Somme.

15 March 1917
Abdication of Tsar Nicholas II of Russia.

6 April 1917
The USA declares war on Germany.

20–22 November 1917
Battle of Cambrai.

3 March 1918
Treaty of Brest-Litovsk.

21 March–18 July 1918
German 'Spring Offensive'.

11 November 1918
Germany agrees to an armistice. The war ends.

18 January–28 June 1919
Versailles Peace Conference in Paris.

Key Topics

Why did the Schlieffen Plan fail?

- The Schlieffen Plan was the German strategy designed to counter the threat of fighting a war on two fronts, against both France and Russia. The plan aimed to knock France out of the war within 42 days and then attack Russia before it had time to mobilise fully.
- The key to the plan's success was a surprise attack through Belgium, rather than along the heavily fortified French–German border.
- **Alfred von Schlieffen**'s plan was a gamble that met a number of unexpected obstacles in 1914:
  - The Russian army mobilised in ten days, not the expected three months.
  - The German advance was too swift for adequate supplies or communication lines to keep up.
  - The Belgians refused to allow the German army to pass through their country without a fight.
  - Britain unexpectedly entered the war.
  - The French army fought with enormous determination and even hired taxis to provide supplies.
  - Von Schlieffen overestimated the endurance of the soldiers who had to march up to 40 miles (60 km) per day as well as fight. By the fourth day the plan was already behind schedule.
- Von Schlieffen's plan was never fully implemented because **General von Moltke** changed the plan in 1914.

Why was there a stalemate on the Western Front?

- By October 1914 British and French counter attacks halted the advance of the Germans and a **stalemate** occurred.
- As a result both sides dug trenches to secure the land they held against attack. By 18 October 1914 the German army faced the Belgian, British and French across a 350 mile (560 km) front line that stretched from Nieuport in Belgium to Basel in Switzerland.
- Successful advances from either side were difficult for a number of reasons:
  - Machine-guns and rapid fire rifles destroyed infantry attacks.
  - Barbed wire and **artillery shells** made **No Man's Land** virtually impossible to cross.
  - Generals on both sides were inexperienced in this new warfare. **General Haig** still believed cavalry (soldiers mounted on horses) would be the decisive factor in the war, whilst French soldiers wore brightly coloured uniforms with highly polished buttons!
  - The newly dug trenches and support lines meant that each side could replace large numbers of casualties or provide ammunition for many years.

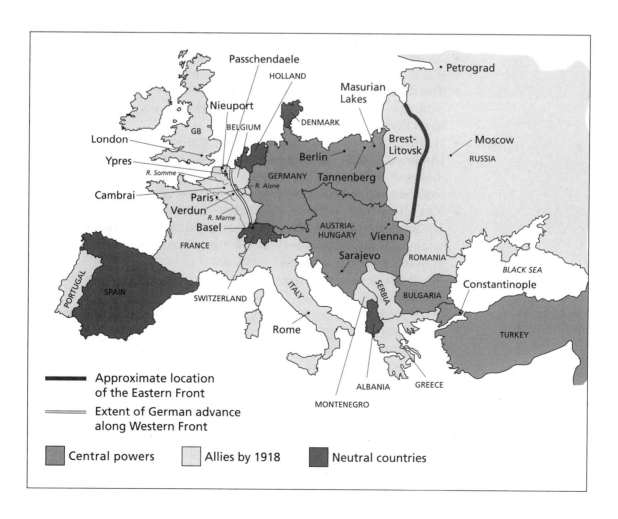

What do I Know?

1 What did the success of the Schlieffen Plan depend on?
2 What surprises did the German attacks of 1914 encounter?
3 Who changed the Schlieffen Plan in 1914?
4 What was each side forced to construct along a 350 mile (560 km) long No Man's Land?
5 Which British general believed the cavalry charge would bring about an Allied victory?

My score ....

Key Topic

What was the nature of 'trench warfare'?

- Soldiers on both sides shared a similar experience. Fear of gas, snipers, shells and attacks across No Man's Land meant a soldier was unable to relax whilst at the front.
- Unlike the German soldiers, British soldiers were given adequate, but dull, food and drink. Many soldiers from working-class areas actually enjoyed a far better diet.
- The average British soldier expected front line duty for one week in every four. The remainder was spent in support trenches awaiting orders.
- The temporary nature of Allied trenches meant soldiers were exposed to the weather. Soldiers endured snow, frost and rain in winter; or dust, flies and sweltering heat in the summer.
- A combination of freezing and damp conditions led to painful diseases such as 'trench foot' and 'trench mouth'.
- The overwhelming experience of a soldier was boredom; most front line soldiers saw little action, apart from occasional and short-lived attacks.
- In the midst of a battle the horrors of war were very apparent. Unburied bodies, many grossly disfigured and torn, lay rotting and unburied among the soldiers. Rats and weasels stalked the trenches and fed from the remains of the dead.
- Not surprisingly, self-injury to escape the trenches was not rare, whilst thousands of soldiers suffered a psychological breakdown commonly known as **shell shock**. Sadly, some victims of this condition were executed as cowards.
- Much of the misery of trench warfare has been blamed on General Haig.
- Many soldiers and some historians today believed Haig allowed thousands of men to risk their lives in futile and bloody attacks, for example the battles at the Somme or Passchendaele. When Haig eventually visited the muddy battlefield at Passchendaele he exclaimed, 'Good God, did we really send men to fight in that?'

The war at sea

- The only major sea battle of the war was the Battle of Jutland between 31 May and 1 June 1916. A total of 250 ships were involved in a two day battle that resulted in three British battleship losses to Germany's two.

- This confrontation led the German High Seas Fleet to remain largely in port for the rest of the war. After the Battle of Jutland the German navy turned its attention instead to its **U-boat** campaign.

The Gallipoli Campaign

- In November 1914 **Winston Churchill** suggested an attack on the Turkish capital, Constantinople (now Istanbul), through the Dardanelles Straits.
- It was hoped that such an attack would lead to the fall of Turkey (one of the **Central Powers**) and would encourage Romania, Greece and Bulgaria to join the war on the Allies' side.
- The Gallipoli Campaign took place in four stages:
  1 February 1915: Allied ships attempted but failed to mine sweep the Dardanelles Straits.
  2 March 1915: Allied ships attacked Turkish positions high on the mountains either side of the Dardanelles Straits and destroyed four Turkish forts. However, six Allied battleships were either destroyed or badly damaged in this attack.
  3 April 1915: The Allied forces, led by Sir Ian Hamilton, launched land invasions along the Gallipoli Peninsula. Poor reconnaissance, sloppy planning and a month's delay in launching the next attack meant the Allies failed to force the Turks out of their well fortified hill-top positions.
  4 October 1915: Hamilton was sacked and replaced by Sir Charles Monro. Within two weeks he decided to evacuate the Peninsula: a two-month operation that was the most successful part of the entire operation as no Allied soldiers were killed during the retreat.

What do I Know?

1 What is shell shock?
2 Which First World War battles are particularly remembered for their high casualties?
3 What was the only major sea battle of the First World War?
4 Why was an Allied attack on Turkey organised in early 1915?
5 Give three reasons why the Allies were unable to conquer the Gallipoli Peninsula in 1915.

My score ………

Key Topic

What was the impact of new technology?

- The First World War has often been described as the first modern war because victory was less reliant on troop numbers and more dependent on how fast each side could manufacture new technologies to support the war effort.

Gas	• The Germans first used gas on the Western Front in April 1915. By 1918 25 per cent of all shells fired by both sides contained poisonous gases. • Chlorine, phosgene and mustard gas were used either to destroy the respiratory system or act as an irritant on eyes and skin. • Despite the fear of gas attacks soldiers soon learned to cope using basic but effective gas masks made out of rubber. • 3 per cent of soldiers killed on the Western Front were poisoned by gas attacks.
Tanks	• The first tanks were used by the British in September 1916 at the Battle of the Somme. • The potential of the tanks was revealed at the Battle of Cambrai between 20 and 22 November 1917 when over 400 Allied Mark IV tanks successfully broke German lines and pushed the enemy back five miles (8 km). • The advantage was lost however when the Allies were unable to keep up with the gains made by the new machines. • Tanks were more successfully used in the final months of the war, particularly at the Battle of Amiens. • Many tanks broke down. Only 25 tanks were still in action after the Battle of Amiens. It was not until the Second World War that the full advantages of the tank were understood and utilised.
Aircraft	• Aircraft did not directly influence the outcome of the war. At first aeroplanes and air balloons were used for **reconnaissance** over enemy positions on the battlefields or out at sea. • As the war progressed aircraft were used in attacks on both sides. Germany's five 'Zeppelins' wounded or killed 1400 British civilians in attacks over Great Yarmouth, Scarborough and London during the war. 2500 Germans were attacked in similar air raids. • **Dogfights** took place in the skies above the Western Front. By 1917 aeroplanes were either equipped with fitted or hand held machine-guns. Famous pilots or 'aces' like the German Baron von Richthofen were treated as daring heroes by the Germans and respected by the Allied airmen. • 50,000 airmen from both sides died during the war.
Guns	• The development of rifles and machine-guns meant infantry attacks, cavalry charges and the use of the bayonet became increasingly impossible. • Even in 1914 the standard British rifle could fire 15 rounds per minute – the Germans believed they were hand held machine-guns! • Similarly a standard machine-gun could fire 1000 rounds per minute – the firepower of 60 riflemen. • The introduction of such technology meant victory could not be secured by outnumbering the enemy alone. One German machine-gunner, at the Battle of the Somme, claimed that whilst he pointed his gun into the British lines he did not even have to aim carefully.
Submarines	• The German navy mainly used submarines – U-boats (Unterseebooten) – in an attempt to disrupt food and munitions supplies across the English Channel and from the USA. • In May 1915 the German High Command suspended its U-boat campaigns following the sinking of the *Lusitania* off the coast of Ireland by a U-boat. 1200 civilians on board this passenger liner drowned, including128 Americans. • From February 1917 the German High Command once again gambled on 'unrestricted submarine warfare' against merchant shipping. They hoped to strangle the Allied war effort. • At first the gamble seemed to be paying off; in the first six months 630,000 tons of supplies were destroyed each month. Britain had just one month of grain left, whilst the British Cabinet discussed how to cope with mass starvation. • By September 1917, however, the introduction of convoys, Q-ships and sea mines cut the number of Allied shipping losses from 25 per cent to just 1 per cent of all Atlantic traffic.

What do I Know?

1 Where were tanks first used successfully?

2 At the start of the war, how did both sides use aircraft?

3 What was the impact of machine-guns and rifles on the battlefield?

4 Why did the Germans introduce U-boat campaigns?

5 How did the Allies limit shipping losses in September 1917?

My score ....

1917: A year of change – part one: the USA enters the war

- On 6 April 1917 the USA finally declared war on Germany. A combination of factors led to this decision.
  - With the abdication of Tsar Nicholas II of Russia in March 1917, the USA now felt that it had to join a war to make 'the world safe for democracy'.
  - Anti-German propaganda resulting from the sinking of the *Lusitania* and exaggerated reports of atrocities committed by German soldiers in Belgium shifted US public opinion in favour of a war against Germany.
  - A telegram from Arthur Zimmermann, Germany's foreign secretary, suggested that Germany was trying to encourage Mexico to invade the USA.
- By late 1918, 2 million US soldiers had landed in Europe, over 100,000 of whom were killed by the end of the war.

1917: A year of change – part two: the Russian defeat

- The arrival of US troops did not make the Germans give up.
- By late 1917 the new Bolshevik government of Russia expected civil war to break out in Russia and was keen to surrender to the German army.
- In March 1918 German and Bolshevik representatives signed the Treaty of Brest-Litovsk. This gave huge areas of land to Germany. It ended the war on the Eastern Front and allowed 1 million German soldiers to be transferred to the Western Front. Germany was now able to concentrate all its forces against the Western Allies.
- The defeat of Russia boosted German morale and enabled **General Ludendorff** to plan Germany's final offensive that would either seal victory or defeat. 'Operation Michael' was launched on 21 March 1918 to try to bring the war to an end before US troops arrived in Europe in large numbers.

Why did Germany lose the First World War?

- On 21 March 1918, 47 German divisions made surprise diagonal attacks against the Allies. 'The Spring Offensive', as it was known, was a last ditch attempt by the Germans to win the war and take advantage of the fresh troops from the Eastern Front.
- The Germans advanced 37 miles (59 km) in just one week. By late May the Germans were just 35 miles (56 km) from Paris and looked on the verge of winning the war.
- The advance was halted at the Second Battle of the Marne (July–September 1918). This was the last major battle of the war and resulted in a general retreat of German forces.
- On 11 November 1918 Germany finally agreed to an **armistice** and hostilities ended.

- In the end Germany believed victory was impossible for a number of reasons:
  - The naval blockades and disrupted harvests had led to food shortages among civilians and soldiers. The problems on the German home front were made worse by power cuts and fewer medical supplies.
  - The Spring Offensive exhausted German soldiers and supplies. At the same time Allied military strength and morale increased daily with the arrival of US troops.
  - Since August 1918 German divisions had been collapsing, surrender was widespread and morale had evaporated.
  - Throughout Germany, soldiers and sailors were mutinying, whilst the threat of communism seemed more menacing to German safety than the Allies. Bread riots and strikes were steadily increasing across Germany.
  - General Ludendorff was also keen to end the war with his army intact and outside Germany's borders.
  - By October 1918 all of Germany's allies had surrendered. Germany was left alone, starving and on the verge of a **civil war**.
- The Germans eventually lost the First World War after three failed gambles: the Schlieffen Plan, the unrestricted U-boat campaign and the Spring Offensive.

Summary Box 1

What do I Know?

1 Give two reasons why the USA declared war on Germany.
2 Why was the defeat of Russia good news for the Germans?
3 What was the 'Spring Offensive'?
4 Which offensive was Germany's last attempt to win the First World War?
5 When was the armistice signed?

My score ....

Key Topic

The Versailles Peace Settlement: a search for peace?

- On 28 June 1919 Germany signed the Treaty of Versailles.
- Immediately the German media and people called the Treaty a 'diktat' (as it was forced upon or dictated to them) and many swore revenge for its harsh terms:
  - **War guilt clause** – this forced Germany to agree it had started the war, was responsible for all the destruction and therefore had to pay for the damage the war had caused.
  - **Land Losses** – Alsace-Lorraine was retuned to France, whilst German land was also given to Belgium, Denmark, Poland and Lithuania. In addition, all German colonies were confiscated.
  - **German Military** – the German army was limited to just 100,000 men and conscription was banned. Germany was not allowed an airforce, submarines or armoured vehicles and was only allowed six battleships. Finally, German troops were prevented from entering the Rhineland.
  - **Reparations** – the final sum was set at £6600 million in 1921. The final instalment was due in 1984. In addition the Saar coalfields were placed under French control for 15 years.
- Germans felt the Treaty was unfair, left them vulnerable to attack and damaged their pride.
- The **reparations** appeared to be an Allied attempt to destroy the German economy.
- Even some of the Allied leaders were unhappy with the Treaty. Woodrow Wilson, the US President, believed the Treaty was too harsh, whilst Georges Clemenceau, the French Prime Minister, believed the Treaty was not harsh enough.

What do I Know?

1 When was the Treaty of Versailles signed?
2 How much did Germany have to pay in reparations?
3 What was the German reaction to the Treaty of Versailles?
4 Who was the US President at the end of the war?

My score ....

Key Words and Names

Alfred von Schlieffen
Architect of the German plan to win a war on two fronts against France and Russia.

Armistice
An agreement to have a ceasefire.

Artillery shells
Exploding bombs launched from large field guns behind the front line.

Central Powers
Collective name given to Germany and its allies; Austria-Hungary, Bulgaria and Turkey.

Civil war
A war fought between people of the same country.

Dogfights
Aerial battles between opposing fighter aircraft.

General Haig
Commander of the entire British forces from late 1915 until the end of the war.

General von Moltke
Commander-in-Chief of the German army from 1906 until late 1914. His modifications to the Schlieffen Plan were blamed for the eventual stalemate.

General Ludendorff
Commander-in-Chief of the German army from 1916 until the end of the war.

No Man's Land
Area of land between the two front lines.

Race for the Sea
The attempt by both sides to outflank the other in an attempt to control north European ports.

Reconnaissance
The assessment of enemy positions, supplies and strength prior to or following an attack.

Reparations
The amounts of money Germany had to pay as punishment for starting the war.

Shell shock
Popular name given to the psychological effects of warfare on soldiers.

Stalemate
Military term used to describe a war in which neither side is able to beat the other.

Winston Churchill
First Lord of the British Admiralty until his resignation following the Gallipoli Campaign.

U-boat
German submarine.

Exam Type Questions

Study the sources and the questions carefully. Attempt the questions yourself, then compare your answers with the answers given and check the examiner's comments.

Source A

> We are able to bring in the wounded who do not lie too far off. But many have long to wait and we listen to them dying. For one we search for two days in vain. Kat thinks he is hurt in the spine or pelvis – his chest cannot be injured otherwise he would not cry out. We crawl out at night but cannot find him. The first day he cries for help, next day he is delirious and cries for his family. In the morning we suppose he has gone to his rest. The dead lie unburied. We cannot bring them all in. If we did we should not know what to do with them.

▲ An account of the war by a German soldier, EM Remarque, in *All Quiet on the Western Front*.

Source B

▲ An advertisement for cigarettes, 1915.

> **1** What can you learn from Source A about trench warfare along the Western Front?

Answer 1

Source A shows how wounded people were often rescued from No Man's Land at night time. Also we learn that the injured sometimes cried out for help and that some were left unburied.

Examiner's
Comments on:
Answer 1

1–2 out of 4
The candidate makes a common mistake. He/she simply summarises the content of the source without identifying inferences. For example, Source A suggests that No Man's Land was too dangerous or chaotic to find survivors; perhaps barbed wire, craters, hundreds of dead bodies and the darkness of night meant searching was impossible. Also the author suggests, in the last sentence, that even if someone was found their fate was much the same since there were few medical facilities.

> **2** How useful is Source B as evidence about a soldier's life in a trench?

Answer 2

The advert gives a very misleading image of what trench warfare was really like. In the picture the soldiers look clean, happy, relaxed and out of danger. Even the scenery looks peaceful and pleasant. The artist probably never visited a trench and was instructed to give a glamorous image of the war to help sales of Mitchell cigarettes. The poster assumes its audience and customers believe that trench warfare was exciting. They hope people will smoke their cigarettes in an attempt to be like the soldiers in the picture. Such posters might have worked in 1915, but by 1916-17 most British people would have realised just how ridiculous this portrayal of trench warfare really was.

**Examiner's
Comments on:
Answer 2**

3 out of 3
The candidate uses his/her knowledge to dismiss the usefulness of this poster as evidence of a soldier's life. In addition the origin and purpose of the source is explored. By doing so the usefulness of the source is clearly judged and dismissed as a poor representation.

> **3** Using Sources A and B and your own knowledge explain why a stalemate broke out along the Western Front.

Answer 3

The introduction of new technology like machine-guns, rapid reloading rifles and aerial reconnaissance meant that both sides were unable to advance against the enemy without suffering enormous casualties. Both sides used machine-gun posts and snipers to make No Man's Land a deadly strip of land. Source A underlines the dangers of entering No Man's Land in an attempt to rescue injured men. Injured soldiers were difficult to find amidst barbed wire and shell craters - caused by the non-stop bombing from both sides.

In addition both sides fully expected to win the war very quickly, using traditional tactics. In the past battles had been fought on open ground with cavalry charges proving decisive. Both sides failed to understand what modern warfare would now be like. This ignorance is shown in Source B. This advert reflects the difficulty most people found imagining what trench warfare would be like. Even the generals on both sides failed to appreciate that cavalry charges were useless and that shells, machine-guns and gas were enough to defend against most attacks.

Examiner's Comments on: Answer 3

4 out of 5

The candidate successfully merges the content of the sources with his/her own knowledge to give a clear answer to the question.

Practice Questions

1. What can you learn from Source B about conditions in a British trench?

   HINT: Do not describe what you see, look for what is inferred or suggested.

2. How useful is Source A as evidence of a soldier's experiences in the First World War?

   HINT: Look at the nature and purpose of this source.

3. Using Sources A and B and your own knowledge explain why many soldiers experienced shell shock as a result of trench warfare.

   HINT: Compare what soldiers expected with what they actually experienced.

2. The Russian Revolution, c.1910–24

Topic Summary

Between 1910 and 1924 Russia had one famine, two wars, three governments, four leaders and a brand new name. By 1924 Russia had been renamed the 'Union of Soviet Socialist Republics' (USSR) and was the first country in the world to be governed along Marxist principles. In these 14 years between 7 and 8 million Russians died as a result of war, famine, freezing weather or terror. Their hardships were a direct result of the struggles between royalists, democrats and Marxists. Each of these opposing forces competed and fought for power in Russia.

What do I Need to Know?

You will need to have a clear understanding of Russia's government and society before the war. In addition you should understand the impact of the First World War on the position of Tsar Nicholas II. Finally you should be able to explain why and how the Bolsheviks seized power from the Provisional Government in 1917 and how they defended their revolution up to 1924.

Key Events

Dates given in this chapter follow the Julian calendar, which the Russians used until 1918. The Julian calendar was 13 days behind the Gregorian calendar, which the rest of Europe followed.

1905
Nicholas II agrees to the 'October Manifesto'. This was the first time that a **Tsar** of Russia had agreed to rule alongside a parliament or 'duma'.

1911
The Russian Prime Minister, **Peter Stolypin**, is assassinated. This event marked the end of the Tsar's reforms.

1 August 1914
Russia declares war on Germany, and later on Austria-Hungary.

September 1915
The Tsar leaves Petrograd to take charge of his army at the front. He leaves his German wife, **Tsarina Alexandra**, in charge. She is advised by **Gregori Rasputin**.

December 1916
The Tsar's cousin, Prince Yusopov, murders Rasputin.

February 1917
Demonstrations and strikes take place on the streets of Petrograd.

2 March 1917
Tsar Nicholas II resigns after his generals encourage him to stand down. The 'Provisional Government' takes over.

April 1917
Along with dozens of the Tsar's opponents, **Lenin** returns from exile in the hope of seizing power through a **revolution**.

May and July 1917
The **Bolsheviks** make two failed attempts to seize power. Lenin goes into hiding whilst the Provisional Government arrests **Trotsky**.

August 1917
General Kornilov, a Tsarist sympathiser, threatens to attack Petrograd and restore the monarchy. The Bolsheviks successfully defeat the Kornilov threat and become heroes within Petrograd.

24–25 October 1917
The Bolsheviks stage a **coup** in Petrograd and declare that Russia has a new government headed by the Bolsheviks.

12 November 1917
The elections to the **Constituent Assembly** take place but are won by the Socialist Revolutionaries. Lenin ignores the result and closes down the Assembly in January – this triggers the Russian **Civil War** (1918–21).

January 1924
Lenin dies following a series of serious strokes. There is no clear successor.

Key Topics

What was Russia like before the First World War?

- Before the First World War Russia was an **autocracy**, ruled by Tsar Nicholas II.
- In the October Manifesto of 1905 the Tsar had granted freedom of speech, universal suffrage and set up a parliament or 'duma'. By 1914, however, he had successfully managed to get the duma to do as they were told. The duma was powerless.
- Most Russian people (80 per cent) were peasant farmers who worked or rented land. They lived with the threat of famine in cramped homes.
- A growing number of Russians were moving into cities like Moscow and the capital, St Petersburg, looking for industrial work. Russian cities became increasingly squalid and overcrowded and a breeding ground for disease. Workers had to work very long hours for very low pay.
- Russia had a very backward agricultural economy in comparison with Western countries such as Britain or Germany.
- The Tsar kept control using a mixture of fear and terror. His secret police force (the **Okhrana**) spied on and arrested opponents of the Tsar, whilst the Russian Orthodox Church told Russians that it was God's will that they love their Tsar.
- Tsar Nicholas II had lots of opponents from all sections of Russian society.

Who were the Tsar's opponents?

- His most extreme opponents were the various **Marxist** groups that existed before the war.
- The biggest and most popular of these groups were the Socialist Revolutionaries (SRs) led by **Victor Chernov**. The SRs were very popular in the countryside amongst the peasants.
- In the cities the Social Democrats which split into two sections, the Bolsheviks and Mensheviks, who were much more popular among the ordinary workers or 'proletariat'.
- The Bolsheviks were led by Lenin and called for the Tsar's government to be replaced by a workers' government.
- All Marxist groups agreed that the Tsar had to go. Some opponents of the Tsar were more moderate. The Kadets, for instance, wanted to keep the Tsar but make the duma much more powerful. They looked to the British system of government as a way forward.
- The Octobrists wanted change to come about using the October Manifesto. They wanted the Tsar to remain powerful but believed the duma should have the power to advise the Tsar. The Octobrists tended to be aristocrats, or very rich Russians, who supported the Tsar.

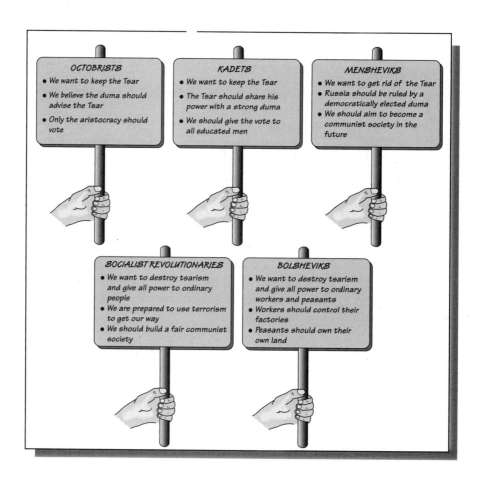

What do I Know?

> 1 Who ruled Russia before the First World War?
> 2 What was the duma?
> 3 What were the key problems in Russia's towns and cities?
> 4 What was the name of the Tsar's secret police force?
> 5 Name the five key opposition groups in Russia.
> 6 What did SRs, Mensheviks and Bolsheviks have in common?
>
> **My score** ....

Key Topic

What was the impact of the First World War on Russia?

- At first the war made the Tsar very popular because most Russians believed they had to support their leader in times of war.
- The Tsar knew that going to war was a gamble. If Russia won, the Tsar's popularity would be assured, but if it lost it would be a different story.
- By early 1915 Russia had experienced massive military losses at the battles of Tannenberg and the Masurian Lakes.
- Successful German industry meant that its army was well supplied and able to destroy the badly equipped Russian army.
- The situation was so bad by September 1915 that the Tsar took personal charge of the army at the front. This meant that, from this point on, all military disasters and the effects of the war were blamed directly on the Tsar.
- The situation in St. Petersburg (renamed 'Petrograd' in 1914) and Moscow worsened towards the end of 1916 as there was plenty of food in the countryside but not enough trains to transport the food into the cities. The result was shortages, inflation, queues and strikes.
- While the Tsar was at war his German wife, Alexandra, was left in charge. She was accused of being a spy and her relationship with Rasputin further destroyed the reputation and respect of the royal family.

Summary Box 1

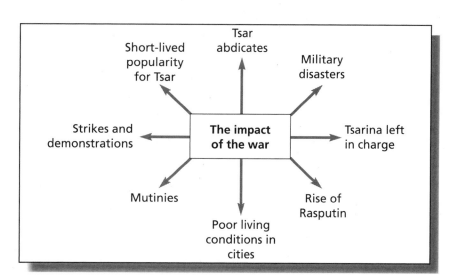

- Rasputin claimed to be able to help her son's haemophilia and used this influence over Alexandra to get ministers sacked or appointed.
- By early 1917 the situation was critical. The army lacked basic supplies, thousands of soldiers had deserted, workers went on strike and even the Tsar's own generals refused to support him.

Why did the Tsar abdicate?

- The Tsar finally resigned (abdicated) on 2 March 1917 when he realised that he no longer had the support of his generals and finally accepted that **mutiny** had spread throughout his army.
- The Tsar had continually overestimated his popularity and refused to acknowledge the suffering of his people.
- His wife's letters from Petrograd suggested that the city was running as normal. Tsar Nicholas refused to believe **Mikhail Rodzianko**'s more accurate description of the situation in Petrograd.
- The military blunders in the First World War, along with the misery in the cities, finally destroyed the Russian people's belief that the Tsar was able to run the country.
- Support for radical Marxist groups like the Social Revolutionaries and the Bolsheviks had grown during the war.
- Even the Tsar's loyal supporters were fed up with him, largely because of the scandal caused by Rasputin's influence over the Tsarina.
- No single event caused the Tsar to abdicate. His style of autocratic government was out of date in the modern world. Even before the war the Tsar was unpopular with a growing number of Russians. In many ways the war may have acted as a catalyst, i.e. the First World War speeded up the Tsar's downfall.

What do I Know?

1 Why did the Tsar leave Petrograd in September 1915?
2 How did the war affect Russia's cities?
3 Give three reasons why some Russians lost respect for the Russian royal family.
4 Which groups found increased support during the war?
5 When did the Tsar abdicate?

My score ....

Key Topic

Why did the Provisional Government lose power?

- When the Tsar abdicated it was unclear who was in charge. Members of the duma assumed they were now in power and declared a Provisional Government; they promised democratic elections for the following November.

- However, the Provisional Government was only really in charge in Petrograd and gradually lost control of Russia's army.
- Throughout the rest of Russia, soldiers, sailors, workers and farmers set up small local governments called 'soviets'. These soviets ignored the Provisional Government and tried to rule independently in their own region. The Petrograd Soviet was the most important one.
- The Provisional Government could have won the support of the Russian people had they ended the war with Germany, redistributed land to the peasants or ensured food was transported into the cities. They failed to deliver these three key demands of the Russian people.
- In April 1917 Lenin returned from Finland and set about getting rid of the Provisional Government and replacing it with a new Bolshevik government.
- The Bolsheviks became increasingly popular in Petrograd itself promising 'peace, bread and land'.
- General Kornilov attempted to overthrow Kerensky, the Prime Minister, in September 1917. Kornilov was defeated but Kerensky was forced to ask the Bolsheviks for support. This made the Bolsheviks even more popular than before and left them with a huge supply of weapons. The Bolsheviks took control of the Petrograd Soviet.
- By October 1917 Leon Trotsky, Chairman of the Military Committee of the Petrograd Soviet, had masterminded a plan to take power in Petrograd. On 24–25 October the Provisional Government's headquarters at the Winter Palace were stormed and the Bolsheviks took power.
- The Winter Palace was left virtually undefended, demonstrating how very little people cared about the survival of the Provisional Government.

What do I Know?

1 Who took control of Russia after the Tsar's abdication?
2 Why was this new government's authority threatened throughout Russia?
3 What were the three key demands of the Russian people?
4 Which group became the rulers of Russia in 1917?
5 Which person organised the October 1917 coup in Petrograd?

My score ....

Key Topic

The Russian Civil War, 1918–21

- The October 1917 revolution left the Bolsheviks in control of Petrograd. Despite the Bolsheviks' popularity in Moscow and other major towns, most Russians were keen supporters of the Social Revolutionaries.

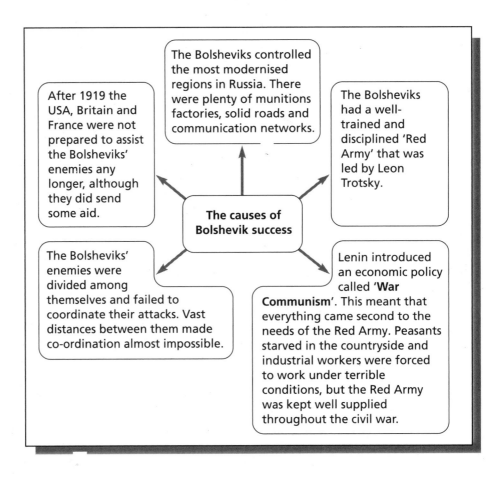

After 1919 the USA, Britain and France were not prepared to assist the Bolsheviks' enemies any longer, although they did send some aid.

The Bolsheviks controlled the most modernised regions in Russia. There were plenty of munitions factories, solid roads and communication networks.

The Bolsheviks had a well-trained and disciplined 'Red Army' that was led by Leon Trotsky.

The causes of Bolshevik success

The Bolsheviks' enemies were divided among themselves and failed to coordinate their attacks. Vast distances between them made co-ordination almost impossible.

Lenin introduced an economic policy called '**War Communism**'. This meant that everything came second to the needs of the Red Army. Peasants starved in the countryside and industrial workers were forced to work under terrible conditions, but the Red Army was kept well supplied throughout the civil war.

- Between 1918 and 1921 the Bolsheviks had to defend their revolution and spread their power right across Russia. This period has become known as the 'Russian Civil War.' The 'Whites', the Bolsheviks' enemies, included members of the Tsar's army, the Czech Legion, Poles, Cossacks and Ukrainians.
- By 1921 the Bolsheviks had secured victory and were securely in power throughout Russia. This was achieved in a number of ways as shown in the flow chart above.
- In July 1918, the Whites approached Ekaterinberg, where the Tsar and his family were being held. It is thought that the Tsar and his family were shot in the basement of the house. Their bodies were dumped in a deep grave before acid and fire were used to try and hide the evidence of their murder.

Bolshevik Policies 1918–24

- This period in Russian history was dominated by the impact of the Russian Civil War.
- War Communism resulted in a famine that killed 5 million people by 1921 and meant that industrial workers continued to live in the misery they had experienced during the First World War.

- To ensure the survival of the revolution, Lenin set up his own secret police force known as the Cheka. By 1924 up to 0.5 million Russians had been murdered by the Cheka. They were accused of many crimes such as being 'traitors', 'enemies of the revolution' or 'enemies of the state', whilst many peasants were executed for being 'hoarders'.
- Lenin supported this terror. He said that the Bolsheviks should hold power 'at all costs'.
- When the sailors in Kronstadt mutinied against Lenin's harsh policies in March 1921, Lenin dropped War Communism in favour of the more popular **New Economic Policy** (NEP).
- The New Economic Policy was a shift back to limited capitalism and in fact helped Russia recover from years of war and famine.
- By 1924 Russia had been given a new name, the Union of Soviet Socialist Republics (USSR) and had introduced a 'one-party state' where only communism was permitted. Even though Lenin claimed that the USSR had the first truly democratic constitution, he held as much power and influence as the Tsar ever did.
- When Lenin died in January 1924 he left no clear successor. In the four years that followed there began a power struggle that eventually resulted in Joseph Stalin assuming full power by 1928.

What do I Know?

1 Which groups fought against the Bolsheviks in the Russian Civil War?
2 Who led and trained the 'Red Army'?
3 What was the name of Lenin's secret police force?
4 Which economic policy was introduced by Lenin to ensure victory in the civil war?
5 What did Russia become known as from 1924?

My score ....

Key Words and Names

Autocracy
This was the style of government preferred by the Tsar. This is when a monarch, like a tsar, emperor or king, rules all by themself.

Bolsheviks
Marxist party led by Lenin and later by Stalin.

Victor Chernov
Leader of the Socialist Revolutionaries. Like Lenin he was a Marxist and wished to overthrow the tsarist government.

Civil war
A war between people of the same country.

Constituent Assembly
A democratically elected body given the task of drawing up a new Russian constitution (i.e. laws and rules).

Coup
An armed take-over of a government.

General Kornilov

Tsarist sympathiser who led the failed attack on the Provisional Government in August 1917.

Lenin

Leader of the Bolsheviks.

Marxism

Based on the teachings of Karl Marx. He believed that society evolved towards power and wealth being equally distributed among the 'proletariat' (working classes).

Mutiny

When soldiers and sailors refuse to follow the orders of their superiors.

New Economic Policy

A policy which saw a return to a more free market capitalist economy.

Nicholas II

The last Tsar of Russia, of the house of Romanov.

Okhrana

This was the name of the Tsar's secret police force used to spy on and arrest opponents.

Gregori Rasputin

Mysterious monk whose alleged magical powers allowed him access to the Tsar's family. He may also have influenced decisions made by the Tsarina whilst the Tsar was away at the war front.

Revolution

When the government of a country is completely changed.

Mikhail Rodzianko

The leader of the duma throughout the First World War.

Peter Stolypin

The Tsar's prime minister from 1906–11. He was a wise reformer and created a significant boom in the Russian economy.

Trotsky

Bolshevik leader who masterminded the October Revolution and civil war victories.

Tsar

This derives from the Roman word 'caesar' or 'emperor'.

Tsarina Alexandra

Tsar Nicholas' German wife.

War Communism

This was designed to help the Bolsheviks gain victory in the civil war. Grain was confiscated from the peasants and factories were ordered to produce armaments.

Exam Type Questions

Study the sources and questions carefully. Attempt the questions yourself, then compare your answers with the answers given and check the examiner's comments.

Source A

> Lynch law, the destruction of homes and shops, jeering at and attacks on officers, unauthorised arrests, seizures and beatings were recorded every day by tens and hundreds. In the country, burnings and destruction of country houses became more frequent. Military discipline collapsed. There were masses of deserters. The soldiers, without leave, went off home in great floods. They filled all the trains, kicked out the passengers and threatened the entire transport system.

▲ **An account of an eyewitness who was in Petrograd in 1917.**

Source B

▲ **A 1930s painting of the storming of the Winter Palace by Sokolov-Skayla.**

> **1** What can you learn from Source A about the situation in Petrograd in 1917?

Answer 1

Source A suggests that Petrograd was in chaos and the situation appeared to be getting even worse. The looting, attacks on the police and the mutiny or desertion of soldiers all suggest the Provisional Government had lost control of the situation and were perhaps about to be overthrown. The source gives the impression that the Provisional Government did not have a single supporter and the whole of Petrograd was united in its hatred of the government.

Examiner's Comments on: Answer 1

3 out of 4

The candidate avoids summarising the content of the source and instead pulls out the clues that Petrograd looked to be on the verge of an uprising against the Provisional Government.

> **2** How useful is Source B as evidence about the Bolsheviks' storming of the Winter Palace.

Answer 2

The painting suggests that the Bolsheviks' storming of the Winter Palace was a major military event that was supported by vast numbers of people. The presence of the canon and the waving flag give the impression of a battlefield and the whole scene feels like a rousing tribute to the Bolsheviks' eventual victory. However the painting was completed in the 1930s when all art forms were censored and encouraged to glorify the Bolshevik revolution. This would suggest the painting is propaganda and therefore an inaccurate representation of the storming of the Winter Palace. The source is not useless however; it does give us a clear idea of how the Bolsheviks wanted the event to be remembered.

Examiner's Comments on: Answer 2

3 out of 3

The candidate summarises how the painting portrays the storming and then successfully judges its usefulness by references to the painting's origin and purpose. The candidate understands the limitations of this source but ends with a valid comment on why the source is useful, despite its inaccuracies.

> **3** Using Sources A and B and your own knowledge explain why the Provisional Government lost power in 1917.

Answer 3

Source A suggests that the Provisional Government had lost control over both the army and the people. The attacks on country houses indicate how peasants began violently to take the wealth from the rich landowners and aristocracy – rather than wait for their government to do it for them. Both the workers and the army had begun to revolt against the Provisional Government by deserting or ignoring the laws of the government. Whilst Source B would suggest that the people of Petrograd united in an attack on the Provisional Government's headquarters, it was actually supported by less than one hundred loyal Bolsheviks – Lenin was not even there!

The chaos and disorder shown in Sources A and B were due to the disastrous decisions made by the Provisional Government. The decision to continue the war was deeply unpopular amongst both the soldiers and city workers, who continued to suffer from rationing, inflation and strikes. Also, the Provisional Government's failure to distribute land, leaving it in the hands of the rich landowners, lost support among Russia's peasants – who formed 80 per cent of the population. In addition, Lenin's return to Petrograd in April 1917 signalled the beginning of the Bolsheviks' attempts to gain power through propaganda and attempted coups. When the Bolsheviks finally stormed the Winter Palace (Source B) and seized power the Provisional Government hardly put up a fight at all – no-one was prepared to die in its defence.

Examiner's Comments on: Answer 3

5 out of 5

The candidate makes a clear attempt to answer the question fully by combining evidence from both sources and the introduction of new background knowledge.

Practice Questions

1. What can you learn from Source B about the storming of the Winter Palace by the Bolsheviks?
   HINT: Study what everyone *appears* to be doing.
2. How useful is Source A as evidence for why the Provisional Government lost power in Russia?
   HINT: Look at the nature, origin and purpose of this source.
3. Using Sources A and B and your own knowledge explain how the Bolsheviks became the new government of Russia between 1917 and 1921.
   HINT: Combine your understanding of how the Bolsheviks exploited the failures of the Provisional Government and showed determination in holding onto power.

3. Depression and the New Deal: The USA, 1929–41

Topic Summary

The Wall Street Crash brought a sudden end to US prosperity and plunged the USA into a 12-year economic depression that saw unemployment peak at 15 million. 5 million people were made homeless and farmers suffered as a result of overproduction and falling prices. From 1933, Roosevelt's 'New Deal' attempted to use the power and wealth of the Federal Government to tackle the effects of the Great Depression and rebuild American wealth and prosperity. Whilst historians disagree on the effectiveness of the New Deal, all agree that it finally took the Second World War to pull the USA out of the Great Depression.

What do I Need to Know?

You will need to be aware of the causes and consequences of the Great Depression. In addition you will need to understand how Hoover and Roosevelt attempted to boost the US economy and be able to assess how successful each president was.

Key Events

1922
Fordney-McCumber Tariff introduced.

July 1926
Unemployment drops to 1 million.

24 October 1929
'Black Thursday', later known as the start of the Wall Street Crash.

4 March 1933
Roosevelt becomes the President of the USA.

March–June 1933
President Roosevelt's first '**100 Days**'.

1933
The FCA, AAA, NIRA, TVA, CWA, PWA and CCC are established to tackle economic recovery and unemployment (see page 34).

1935
The NLRB, WPA and SSA are set up to tackle unemployment and to offer relief and better welfare provision for all.

July 1937
Unemployment falls to under 7.5 million.

December 1941
Following the Japanese attack on Pearl Harbor, the USA enters the Second World War.

Key Topics

What were the causes of the Wall Street Crash?

- The US economy boomed in the 1920s. Millions of Americans spent millions of dollars on new electrical goods, houses and cars. Unemployment fell and the standard of living for the average American rose considerably.
- Millions of Americans gambled on the New York Stock Exchange on Wall Street. Between 1927 and 1929 the average share price rose 300 per cent. This meant that $10 invested in 1927 was worth $30 in 1929.
- However, this prosperity was built on very shaky foundations!
  - In 1922 the Fordney-McCumber Tariff raised import duties on goods coming into the USA and slowed down trade between the USA and Europe.
  - This meant that imports were more expensive which encouraged Americans to buy US goods.
  - By the late 1920s most people had already bought everything they needed; factories were fast running out of customers.
  - The prosperity was not shared equally among Americans; 71 per cent of Americans did not have a **disposable income**. This meant that they were unable to purchase goods.
  - Americans had borrowed too much money. Goods were bought on hire purchase (**HP**). Shares were bought 'on the margin', in the hope that share prices would keep on rising.
- By mid 1929 factory production had completely outstripped demand. In simple terms, the shops could not find enough customers. Factories began to lay off workers and eventually became bankrupt.

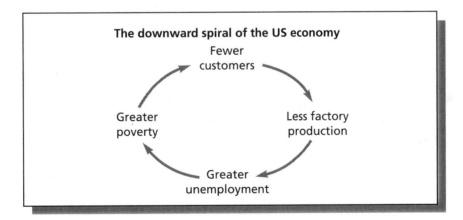

The downward spiral of the US economy

- These bankruptcies led many Americans to lose confidence in the US economy and they began to sell their shares. On 'Black Thursday' (24 October 1929) Wall Street share prices began to collapse.
- By July 1932 average share prices had fallen to just one-eighth of their September 1929 price. In other words, $8 invested in 1929 was worth just $1 by 1932.

- Millions of Americans were caught in a **credit trap**. They had borrowed thousands of dollars to buy shares, homes, household goods and cars. Many now found themselves unemployed with debts they could not possibly hope to pay off.
- American farmers and black agricultural workers did not benefit from the 1920s boom years. Their situation was made even worse in the 1930s because exports had dried up completely, and market prices for livestock and crops had collapsed.
- The Great Depression began.

What do I Know?

> 1 How did many Americans try to make quick profits during the 1920s?
> 2 Why did American factories begin running out of customers by the late 1920s?
> 3 How did Americans pay for shares and electrical goods?
> 4 When did the New York stock market collapse?
> 5 Why did millions of Americans struggle to pay off their debts?
>
> **My score** ....

Key Topic

What was the impact of the Great Depression on US society?

- Between 1929 and 1932, 25,000 American companies went bankrupt and industrial production dropped by 50 per cent.
- By July 1933 up to 15 million Americans were unemployed, while the average family income fell from $2300 to just $1600 a year.
- Over 5000 banks collapsed because companies and individuals could not afford to repay their loans. As a result 9 million Americans lost all their savings.
- Poverty stricken families relied on charity payments of $2–3 per family per week. Soup kitchens, bread queues and temporary settlements for homeless families called '**Hoovervilles**', sprang up in every US state.
- 20 million Americans suffered from malnutrition, whilst 110 people actually died of starvation.
- 5 million Americans, mainly men, became vagrants (hoboes) and wandered around the US looking for work via the railways.
- Church attendance fell dramatically, whilst the prison population rose by 40 per cent. Crimes involving theft rose, but violent crime decreased.
- The richest 5 per cent of Americans were hardly affected at all. Billionaires like John F Kennedy's father sold their shares well before the average American understood that the economy was in trouble.
- Cinema-going was the only boom in the Depression years. Most films were very escapist and avoided social issues. For example, *Snow White and the Seven Dwarfs* (1937), *The Wizard of Oz* (1939) and *Gone With The Wind* (1939).

Summary Box 1

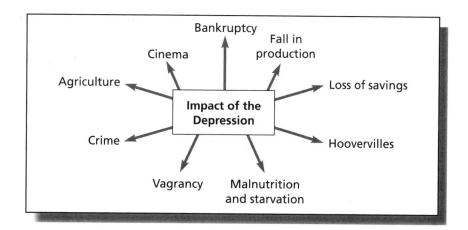

The government's reaction to the Great Depression, 1929–32.

- Herbert Hoover was President during this period. He was a strong advocate of **laissez faire government.**
- Hoover was seen as cold and uncaring by most Americans because he believed in **rugged individualism**, i.e. it was not the responsibility of the national government to relieve poverty:
  - Hoover believed individual cities and local charities should aid the needy.
  - He feared a nation of lazy Americans who relied on government payouts.
- However, Hoover did more than any other president before him to help tackle poverty:
  - He received pledges from big employers to maintain wage levels and avoid redundancies.
  - He initiated **public works programmes**, which created thousands of new jobs.
  - His Federal Farm Board tried to raise agricultural prices and help struggling farmers.
- In the winter of 1931–2 Hoover stepped up his attempts to kick-start the economy by pumping $1.5 billion into new public works programmes and making $300 million available for poverty relief.
- Hoover's attempts to end the Depression did not prevent Franklin Delano Roosevelt's election victory in November 1932.

What do I Know?

1 Why did so many US families find themselves in poverty in the early 1930s?
2 How did the US government try to help poverty stricken Americans up to 1932?
3 What was the only boom industry in the 1930s?
4 Why was President Hoover not prepared to provide welfare for all Americans?
5 In what ways did Hoover attempt to help Americans out of their poverty?

My score ....

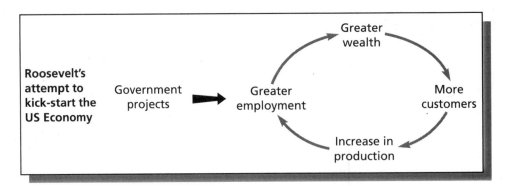

Roosevelt's attempt to kick-start the US Economy → Government projects ➡ Greater employment → Greater wealth → More customers → Increase in production → (back to Greater employment)

Key Topic

What was the 'New Deal'?

- Roosevelt offered poverty stricken America a 'New Deal' to combat the Great Depression.
- Roosevelt believed the Federal Government should use its huge financial resources to kick-start the economy by introducing vast government building projects.
- The New Deal aimed to solve the crises in agriculture and industry, whilst tackling unemployment and providing welfare for suffering Americans.
- Roosevelt set up a number of powerful **alphabet agencies** to tackle the Great Depression (see chart below).

Agriculture: 	**Farm Credit Administration (FCA) 1933.** The government refinanced 20 per cent of farmers' mortgages. Thousands were now able to avoid bankruptcy and eviction. **Agricultural Adjustment Administration (AAA) 1933.** This organised the deliberate destruction of livestock and crops to ensure higher agricultural prices for farmers. For example, 6 million pigs were slaughtered.
Industry: 	**National Industry Recovery Act (NIRA) 1933.** This monitored fair working practices by abolishing child labour and setting minimum working conditions and wages. **Tennessee Valley Authority (TVA) 1933.** The most ambitious and expensive government project of all. It provided for the construction of dams, electrical power stations, fertilisers and homes for the Tennessee Valley region, covering seven states. **National Labour Relations Board (NLRB) 1935.** This guaranteed workers' rights to form and join trade unions.
Unemployment: 	**Civil Works Administration (CWA) 1933.** This created 4 million jobs for people in the public sector. **Public Works Administration (PWA) 1933.** This was a more comprehensive public works programme with $3300 million worth of government funding for dams, bridges, schools, hospitals and other public facilities. **Civilian Conservation Corps (CCC) 1933.** 2.5 million jobs for young men were created in conservation projects. Workers were paid $30 per week on the condition that $25 was sent home to support their families. **Works Progress Administration (WPA) 1935.** This employed a further 8.5 million Americans on 1.5 million public works projects. They included teachers, artists, writers and actors.
Welfare: 	**Social Security Act (SSA) 1935.** A very significant development. It was the first time that the US government took responsibility for providing pensions, unemployment benefits and sick pay for its people. **Fair Labour Standards Act, 1938.** This outlawed child labour and enforced maximum and minimum working hours and pay. A **minimum wage** was also introduced.

What do I Know?

1 How did Roosevelt attempt to help American farmers?
2 How did the New Deal try to protect the American workforce?
3 How did Roosevelt attempt to create millions of new jobs?
4 Which was the US governments' most ambitious project?

My score ………

Key Topic

What role did Roosevelt play in the New Deal?

- When Roosevelt became President on 4 March 1933 he immediately closed all banks until they could prove they were financially secure.
- On 12 March 1933 Roosevelt broadcast his first (of 27) 'fireside chats' and reassured Americans it was safe to deposit their money in reopened banks. Overnight Roosevelt instilled confidence in the banking system. He appeared to be a man who could be trusted!
- In his first **100 Days** as President, Roosevelt pushed 15 **bills** through Congress. This added to a growing feeling that Roosevelt was a man of action and courage.
- At each new presidential election Roosevelt's popularity grew:
  o 1932: 57.8 per cent of the vote.
  o 1936: 60.7 per cent of the vote.
  o 1940: 61.9 per cent of the vote.
- Support for Roosevelt grew particularly among the poor, such as black Americans who valued his relief programmes.

Was there any opposition to Roosevelt and the New Deal?

- The New Deal was increasingly seen as a threat to free enterprise and therefore US capitalism.
- Roosevelt came under increasing criticism from big businesses, the **Supreme Court** and the state governments.
  o Big businesses believed the New Deal involved high taxes and had destroyed 'rugged individualism'.
  o The Supreme Court considered there to have been an illegal growth in presidential and Federal Government power. In 1935 and 1936 it declared the NIRA and the AAA unconstitutional.
  o Many state governments believed Roosevelt was taking away their power and authority.
- Many rich industrialists felt the New Deal made poorer Americans rely on welfare handouts and encouraged a lazy society.
- Others, like Senator Huey P Long, felt Roosevelt ought to 'Share Our Wealth' and actively redistribute the USA's money along socialist principles.

How successful was the New Deal?

Failures

- The New Deal gave little support for **sharecroppers**, small farmers, the rural unemployed or the old.
- Agricultural policies only benefited the wealthier farmers.
- Black Americans and Native Americans were barred from many public works programmes.
- Just 138,000 homes were built in public works programmes.
- Unemployment was still 9.5 million in 1939, 17 per cent of the entire population.
- The USA was the only developed nation that had not recovered from the Great Depression by 1939.

Successes

- Millions of jobs were created through public works schemes.
- Better working conditions and wages were guaranteed under law.
- Workers rights and powers were increased.
- Banks and the stock market were carefully regulated and controlled.
- The welfare state was introduced for the first time.
- Presidential and Federal Government powers were increased. This helped contribute to the successful war effort during the Second World War.
- Roosevelt restored US pride and ensured the preservation of both capitalism and democracy.

- It took the Second World War finally to rid the USA of unemployment and poverty. By 1945 the USA had become an economic superpower. Its people once again enjoyed the highest standard of living in the world and the USA became the richest nation on Earth.

What do I Know?

1 How did Roosevelt gain Americans' trust?
2 Amongst which group did Roosevelt find most popularity?
3 Which groups criticised Roosevelt's policies?
4 Why did some Americans oppose welfare handouts?
5 Who believed Roosevelt had not provided enough welfare handouts?
6 Who did not benefit from the New Deal?
7 Did the New Deal successfully combat unemployment?
8 Give three benefits of the New Deal for the US people.
9 Which event finally brought an end to the Great Depression?

My score ………

Key Words and Names

100 Days
The period at the beginning of Roosevelt's presidency, when 15 new bills were rushed through Congress in an attempt to halt the Great Depression. It has now become a common way of measuring any new leader's first three months in power.

Alphabet agencies
Nickname given to the numerous organisations created throughout the New Deal.

Bill
A proposed change to a country's laws. If passed by a parliament or Congress, a bill becomes an 'act'.

Credit trap
The stock market collapse often meant that Americans' debts were greater than the value of the shares, cars and homes they had bought on credit.

Disposable income
The money a family has available to spend on luxuries (like radios) after essential goods (like bread) have been bought.

Fordney-McCumber Tarriff
A trade barrier designed to make imports too expensive for Americans to purchase. It resulted in tariffs imposed by other countries that slowed US exports.

Hoovervilles
Makeshift towns built by homeless Americans during Hoover's presidency.

HP
Hire purchase. This is a method of paying for shares or goods by borrowing money and paying the loan back over a period of months or years in addition to any interest charges.

Laissez faire government
The belief that an economy is more effective if it is left unregulated and uncontrolled by the government.

Minimum wage
An attempt to guarantee a basic standard of living through decent pay.

Public works programmes
Enormous construction projects that provide public services and work for the unemployed. For example, dams, bridges, schools and parks were built.

Rugged individualism
A belief, linked to laissez faire government, that US people should not depend on the government for aid.

Sharecroppers

Poor farmers who rented a small plot of land from a landlord. They usually gave half of their produce to the landlord in return for a home, mule and seeds.

Supreme Court

The USA's highest court. It has the power to overturn any new laws passed by the US Congress or President.

Exam Type Questions

Study the sources and questions carefully. Attempt the questions yourself, then compare your answers with the answers given and check the examiner's comments.

Source A

▲ A homeless family outside their makeshift home in 1937.

Source B

> Guys like us, that work on ranches, are the loneliest guys in the world. They got no family. They don't belong no place. They come to a ranch an' work up a stake and then go inta town and blow their stake, and the first thing you know they're pounding their tail on some other ranch. They ain't got nothing to look ahead to ... OK. Bring your bundle over here by the fire. It's gonna be nice spleepin' here. Look'in up, and the leaves. Don't build up no more fire. We'll let her die down.

▲ An extract from John Steinbeck's novel, *Of Mice And Men*.

1 What can you learn from Source A about the impact of the Great Depression on Americans?

Answer 1

Source A suggests that Americans were forced into a life of poverty and boredom by the Great Depression. The family looks exhausted and unclean, whilst the children lack shoes. The father looks like he has given up hope for the future and looks with sadness at his children.

Examiner's Comments on: Answer 1

3 out of 4

The candidate spots a number of clues in the photograph to make inferences about the quality of life of the family and the attitude of the father in particular. However, to get full marks the candidate needs to provide more background information about the impact of the Great Depression on American people.

2 How useful is Source B as evidence about the impact of the Great Depression on US people?

Answer 2

The novel depicts the life of agricultural workers who were forced to wander around the USA searching for work. The extract suggests that most slept rough and felt they had no future whatsoever. The extract seems to suggest the story is told through the eyes of one person. The novel therefore presents the views of one character whose outlook and situation may not have been typical of other people at that time. The author was probably trying to draw attention to the plight and misery of the Great Depression and is therefore likely to give a very negative portrayal of life to make a point. The extract is not unrealistic however; millions of Americans were forced to live this way.

Examiner's Comments on: Answer 2

3 out of 3

The candidate successfully explores the nature and purpose of the source in full. This enables a careful judgement of the extent to which the extract represents the typical experience of an American at this time.

> **3** Using Sources A and B and your own knowledge explain how the Great Depression affected US society in the 1930s.

Answer 3

Source A shows how typical families were forced into 'Hoovervilles' as they waited for new jobs. The result being that families lacked adequate food and clothing. Many simply lost hope and resigned themselves to a life of poverty. Source B presents a biased yet realistic view of one migrant worker who had lost all hope for the future. The source suggests that families were broken apart ('they got no family') and people constantly wandered around in search of work ('they got no place'). Unlike the family in Source A the characters in Source B slept rough next to campfires, again pointing out the poverty many faced.

Although both sources give the perspective of just a few individuals, they represent the typical experiences faced by Americans. During the 1930s 5 million Americans wandered round looking for work, most did not have a job long enough to bother building a makeshift house. The worldwide depression destroyed the demand for agricultural exports and therefore farmers were left without anyone to buy their produce. Millions of farmers became debt ridden and could not afford to employ labourers. Even the efforts of the Agricultural Adjustment Act (1933) failed to save the poorest farmers, or 'sharecroppers', who tended to be the ones who left in search of work.

Examiner's Comments on: Answer 3

4 out of 5

Both sources are used well to pull out answers to the question. In the second paragraph the limitations of the sources are discussed. The candidate successfully builds on inferences made from the sources by selecting appropriate knowledge to give a clear answer to the question.

Practice Questions

1. What can you learn from Source B about how the Great Depression affected the attitudes of Americans?

   HINT: Look for phrases that suggest the character has lost hope.

2. How useful is Source A as evidence for poverty during the Great Depression?

   HINT: Suggest possible origins and and purposes of the source.

3. Using Sources A and B and your own knowledge explain why the New Deal was so popular amongst the USA's poorest citizens.

   HINT: Think about elements of the New Deal that dealt with the problems seen in sources A and B.

4. Nazi Germany, 1930–9

Topic Summary

The 1929 Wall Street Crash provided Hitler with the opportunity to win the support of the German people. Once in power Hitler set about destroying the democratic system that brought him to power and building a totalitarian government in its place. Hitler's Germany destroyed all opposition and began to remove 'undesirable' sections from German society. By 1939, through a mixture of economic stability, rising prosperity, propaganda and terror, Hitler's authority was secure and his people devoted to his vision of a new Germany.

What do I Need to Know?

You will need to know who Hitler and the Nazis were and how they finally came to power by 1933. In addition you need to understand how Hitler, once in power, firmly established his dictatorship and how he treated women, children, minorities and opponents.

Key Events

October 1929
The Wall Street Crash.

July 1932
The Nazis poll 13.7 million votes and become the biggest party in the **Reichstag**.

30 January 1933
Hitler becomes **Chancellor**.

27 February 1933
The Reichstag Fire.

5 March 1933
The Nazis win another election and receive 44 per cent of the national vote.

23 March 1933
The Enabling Act is passed by a two-thirds majority of the German Reichstag.

1 April 1933
Boycott of all Jewish businesses.

2 May 1933
All trade unions banned.

14 July 1933
All opposition parties and groups officially banned. Germany therefore becomes a **one-party state**.

30 June 1934
The Night of the Long Knives.

2 August 1934
President Hindenburg dies. As a result Hitler becomes Führer (leader).

September 1935
The Nuremberg Laws.

9–10 November 1938
'Kristallnacht', the 'Night of Broken Glass'.

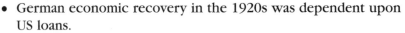

Key Topics

What was the impact of the Wall Street Crash on Germany?

- German economic recovery in the 1920s was dependent upon US loans.
- After the Wall Street Crash these loans were ended, repayments were demanded and world trade collapsed. Germany had borrowed a lot of money so was badly affected by the Crash.
- Falling exports and bankruptcies led to unemployment rising to 6.5 million by mid-1932.
- Thousands became homeless and ended up living in tent cities in public parks. The nation's diet became restricted and led to an increase in malnutrition and infant mortality.

What were the key beliefs of the Nazi Party?

- The Nazi Party started as a gathering of ex-soldiers who hated the Weimar Government. They believed Germans had been 'stabbed in the back' by the politicians who had signed the armistice in 1918 and the Treaty of Versailles in 1919. They wanted a return to a more authoritarian government. They particularly hated communists, Jews and democrats.
- The Nazis hated democracy, and as fascists believed the country needed a dictator who was able to make decisions for the good of all society – they wanted a **dictatorship**.
- They believed in heavy censorship and the elimination of all opposition groups.
- **Adolf Hitler** aimed to reunite all German-speaking people torn apart by the Treaty of Versailles.
- In addition the Nazis wanted to acquire new land or *Lebensraum* for German people.
- The Nazis promoted the idea that Jews and other minority groups were to blame for Germany's problems and should be removed from society.
- The Nazis believed that 'true blooded Germans' or 'Aryans' were the master race and were destined to rule over *Untermenschen* or 'sub-humans' such as Jews, gypsies or Slavs.

Why did the Nazis become so popular in Germany?

- Germany had had a democratic government since the First World War. Hitler was able to convince Germans that the defeat in 1918, the Treaty of Versailles and its effects, hyperinflation in 1923 and the Great Depression were a direct result of weak Weimar governments.
- Hitler convinced ordinary Germans that they needed a single leader who would steer them towards stability and prosperity.
- Hitler also promised revenge for the Treaty of Versailles. His promises to reunite the German people, end reparation payments and revive German wealth attracted enormous numbers of desperate Germans.
- During election campaigns the **SA** ('Sturm Abteilung') effectively intimidated political opponents and voters. The SA successfully forced some Germans to vote for the Nazis or frightened others away from the polling stations.
- The Nazis used successful propaganda campaigns (organised by **Joseph Goebbels**) that took the form of speeches or parades across Germany.
- No single factor brought Hitler to power. However, without the Great Depression, Hitler's charismatic appeal and propaganda campaigns, the Nazi Party might not have been so successful.

Summary Box 1

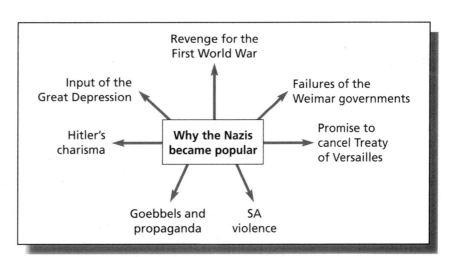

What do I Know?

1 Why was the German economy dependent on the USA by the late 1920s?
2 How many Germans were unemployed by mid-1932?
3 What was *Lebensraum*?
4 Who did the Nazis believe was to blame for Germany's problems?
5 Which Nazi group intimidated the Nazis' opponents?

My score ....

Who started the Reichstag fire?

- On the night of 27–28 February 1933 the Reichstag building was completely destroyed by an arson attack.
- **Marinus Van der Lubbe** was quickly arrested and subsequently executed for the crime.
- Adolf Hitler successfully used the fire to the Nazis' advantage. He convinced President Hindenburg, and many other Germans, that the attack was part of a communist conspiracy to seize power across Germany.
- Hindenberg agreed with Hitler and declared a state of emergency. This allowed Hitler, as Chancellor, to use **Article 48** and rule by decree. With the new elections just one week away, Hitler was able to use his new powers to arrest leading communists, close their newspapers and convince even more Germans that he was the country's only solution to the growing threat of communism.
- The Nazi Party fully exploited the Reichstag fire. This has led many historians to suggest that someone within the Nazi Party (perhaps the Berlin SA leader, Karl Ernst) started the fire and that Van der Lubbe was a scapegoat.
- It is possible that Marinus Van der Lubbe started the fire. He had been a member of the Communist Party and was known to hate German democracy. However it is equally likely that he was completely innocent and that someone within the Nazi Party successfully set him up.

What was the 'Night of the Long Knives'?

- Hitler knew that the only group in Germany that could remove him from power was the German army.
- The German army did not oppose Hitler's rise to power but most generals disliked **Ernst Röhm**, leader of the SA.
- Röhm wanted to merge the SA and the German army and become overall leader. Both the German army and Hitler himself felt very threatened by Röhm's ambitions.
- On the night of 29 June 1934, Ernst Röhm, Karl Ernst and 150 SA leaders (plus another 850 enemies) were murdered by the **SS**.
- In one night Hitler removed all potential opponents and gained the support and trust of the German army.
- From this point, the SA was vastly reduced in size whilst the SS became the most important group within the Nazi Party. Meanwhile, the German army was massively expanded in preparation for war.

1 Who was blamed for the Reichstag Fire?
2 Who gave Hitler the power to rule by decree?
3 Which two groups did Hitler feel threatened by?
4 Who was the leader of the SA?
5 Which two groups benefited from the 'Night of the Long Knives'?

My score ....

Key Topic

How did Hitler take control of Germany?

- Between March 1933 and August 1934 Hitler gradually destroyed democracy in Germany and became an all-powerful dictator:

  28 February 1933
  - Following the Reichstag fire communist leaders were arrested and their newspapers closed down.

  23 March 1933
  - The German Reichstag passed the 'Enabling Act' that gave Hitler the power to rule by decree for four years.

  2 May 1933
  - All trade unions were merged into one. It was called the 'German Labour Front' and was headed by a Nazi. This removed the potential for workers to unite against Hitler.

  14 July 1933
  - All political parties, except the Nazi Party, were banned. Germany became a one-party state.

  30 June 1934
  - The Night of the Long Knives. Threats within the Nazi Party were finally removed whilst the support of the German army was also secured.

  2 August 1934
  - President Hindenburg died aged 85. Hitler merged the posts of chancellor and president and declared himself 'Führer' of Germany. The next day all German soldiers and sailors were required to swear an oath of allegiance to Adolf Hitler.

- In addition to these events Hitler entrusted Joseph Goebbels' 'Ministry of Enlightenment and Propaganda' to use all forms of media, like radio, posters, films and parades, to convince ordinary Germans of the Nazis' greatness and Hitler's ability to rule. The arts were censored and only pro-Nazi plays, art or music were permitted.
- All those who refused to accept Hitler's authority were rounded up and imprisoned in concentration camps such as Dachau.

Did the Nazis improve the German economy?

- Nazi propaganda reminded Germans of their achievements in reducing unemployment from 6 million in 1933 to virtually zero by 1939.
- In addition homelessness was ended whilst the value of exports improved.
- Most of the new jobs that were created were as a result of either massive conscription into the armed forces, or the huge public works schemes that sprang up all over Germany.
- Hundreds of thousands of new jobs were 'created' when women, Jews and other minorities were either forced out or pressurised to resign from their jobs.

- By 1938 the average German worker worked 40 per cent longer than they had in 1928 and did so for 20 per cent less pay!
- German workers rarely complained about this. They were either too afraid or were actually glad to have a steady job with decent pay.
- Workers and their families benefited through the 'Strength Through Joy' (*Kraft durch Freude*) movement. This Nazi-run organisation arranged leisure activities like sports events, camping, concerts, film shows and vacations for all German workers.

What do I Know?

1 Which Act gave Hitler the power to rule by decree for four years?
2 Whose death allowed Hitler to gain more power?
3 Who was placed in charge of propaganda by Hitler?
4 List three ways in which the Nazis created new jobs in the 1930s.
5 Which Nazi organisation provided entertainment for workers and their families?

My score ....

Key Topic

How did the Nazis treat minority groups in Germany?

- Hitler believed that Aryans were the master race or *Herrenvolk*. He saw all other human beings as inferior.
- Minority groups such as Jews, gypsies, physically and mentally handicapped people, homosexuals, communists, tramps, beggars and alcoholics were therefore labelled as *Untermenschen* (sub-human) and were subsequently treated as second-class citizens.
- The Nazis used schools to encourage this idea of a master race through lessons like 'race studies', 'eugenics' or 'health biology'
- Hitler's persecution of the Jews began slowly, but had gathered momentum by the end of the 1930s.
- On 1 April 1933 Hitler declared a boycott of all Jewish shops and businesses.
- In 1935 the Nuremberg Laws removed Jews' civil rights and turned them into official second-class citizens.
- In November 1938 the Nazis organised an all-out attack on Jews throughout Germany on *Kristallnacht* (The Night of Broken Glass). Over 30,000 Jews were arrested and many more saw their homes and businesses destroyed.
- For many Jews this was the last straw; thousands emigrated abroad.
- However, the persecution of the Jews in the 1930s was relatively minor in comparison with the Holocaust which took place during the Second World War.
- Between 1933 and 1939, 240,000 Jews fled Germany.
- Other minority groups faced persecution in similar ways. Thousands were arrested and interned in concentration camps, whilst many others were sterilised so that, according to Hitler, they could not 'pollute German blood'.

How did the Nazis change the lives of German children?

- The Nazis dominated children's lives.
- When they woke up they would listen to Nazi controlled radio stations. School lessons were strictly planned to promote Nazi ideas and Hitler. Evenings and weekends were filled with youth organisation meetings and vacations that combined fun, fitness and indoctrination (brainwashing).
- At school, girls were only taught lessons that encouraged maternal and domestic skills, whilst boys were given lessons that might better prepare them for industry or the armed forces.
- Youth organisations were created for boys and girls from the ages of 4 to 18. Girls could join the 'League of German Maidens' whilst boys could join Hitler Youth.
- The Nazis' Minister of Education said, 'the whole purpose of education is to create Nazis'.

What do I Know?

1 What name did the Nazis give to the German 'master race'?
2 Which minority groups did the Nazis persecute?
3 When did the Nazis organise their first attack on Jewish homes and businesses?
4 What were German boys and girls prepared for by the Nazis?
5 Which youth organisations could German boys and girls join?

My score ....

Key Topic

How did the Nazis view German women?

- During the 1920s women gained greater equality with men in terms of wages, jobs and voting rights.
- However, the Nazis reversed many of the gains women had made. The Nazis preferred women to adopt a more traditional role as a wife and mother. They encouraged a return to these traditional roles by giving women extra money or public awards for having lots of children or leaving their jobs.
- Hitler wrote in *Mein Kampf* that a woman's primary function in life was to produce children. He claimed that, 'childbirth is to women what war is to men'.
- Maternity leave became more financially attractive, whilst contraception and abortions became illegal.
- Many women were sterilised (100,000 by 1937) if they were classed as unfit to be mothers. These included the mentally disabled, hypochondriacs, prostitutes and even the colour blind.
- The Nazis sacked women who were trained as doctors, civil servants, teachers, lawyers or judges.
- Instead women were encouraged to stick to the 'Three K's'; Kinder (children), Kirche (church) and Kuche (kitchen).

Did anyone oppose the Nazi Party?

- Hitler was the head of a totalitarian state. This meant that he was a dictator who did not allow any other opposition.
- Any known opponents were imprisoned and sent to concentration camps. 3 million Germans were imprisoned in such camps by 1939.
- The first opponents were the German Communist Party and the Social Democratic Party.
- Hitler also feared the Centre Party whose supporters were mainly Roman Catholic.
- The Enabling Law of March 1933 allowed Hitler to ban all opposition groups and turn Germany into a one-party state.
- Many young Germans hated Hitler's leadership and control. Often groups like the White Rose, Edelweiss Pirates or the Navajos Gang beat up Hitler Youth boys, wrote anti-Nazi graffiti and distributed leaflets. Many of these young Germans were executed for their opposition.
- Despite this opposition, Hitler did not face any serious threat to his position between 1933 and 1939.
- The biggest single threat in this period came from within the Nazi Party itself. However Hitler used The Night of the Long Knives to destroy the threat from Ernst Röhm.

What do I Know?

1 In what ways did the Nazis treat women as second-class citizens?
2 What did the Nazis believe the primary role of women to be?
3 What do the 'Three K's' stand for?
4 How many Nazi opponents were sent to concentration camps by 1939?
5 How did Hitler turn Germany into a one-party state? (Mention the Enabling Law, Nazi opposition and the economy in your answer.)

Key Words and Names

Article 48
The emergency powers that gave a German chancellor the power to rule by decree when the president declared a 'state of emergency'.

Chancellor
Leader of the German Reichstag; equivalent to the British prime minister.

Dictatorship
A system of government where one person is in complete control of the government, laws and armed forces.

Joseph Goebbels
Minister for Enlightenment and Propaganda. Became Hitler's deputy by the end of the Second World War.

Hindenburg
German President up to 1934. He gave Hitler emergency powers after the Reichstag Fire and failed to recognise the threat Hitler posed to German democracy.

Adolf Hitler
Austrian born leader of the National Socialist German Workers' Party (Nazi Party) from 1921 until his suicide in 1945. German Chancellor from January 1933. Became the 'Führer' from 1934 and created a strong dictatorship.

One-party state
A country that is ruled by a single political party and bans all opposition groups.

President
German head of state. Equivalent to the British monarch.

Reichstag
The German parliament, equivalent to the British House of Commons.

Ernst Röhm
Led the SA until his execution in 1934. He was more revolutionary than Hitler and wanted to take control of the German army.

SA
'Sturm Abteilung', known as 'Stormtroopers' or 'Brown Shirts'. They were the Nazis' own private army. They supported Hitler in his failed 'Beer Hall Putsch' and intimidated opponents in elections between 1930 and 1933. Led by Ernst Rohm until 1934.

SS
Schutz Staffel. Initially Hitler's personal bodyguard; later expanded into military units whilst taking control of state security and concentration camps.

Marinus Van der Lubbe
Dutch youth beheaded for his alleged arson attack on the Reichstag building. The Nazis claimed he was part of a communist conspiracy.

Exam Type Questions

Study the sources and questions carefully. Attempt the questions yourself, then compare your answers with the answers given and check the examiner's comments.

Source A

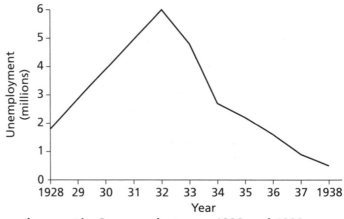

▲ **Unemployment in Germany between 1928 and 1938.**

Source B

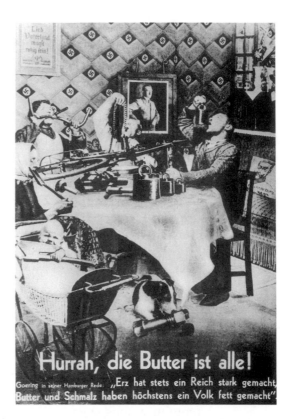

Hurrah, die Butter ist alle!

Goering in seiner Hamburger Rede: „Erz hat stets ein Reich stark gemacht, Butter und Schmalz haben höchstens ein Volk fett gemacht"

▲ **From a banned communist magazine in 1935. The caption reads, 'Hurrah, the butter is all gone'.**

> **1** What can you learn from Source A about the German economy in the 1930s?

Answer 1

The graph shows how unemployment came down from 6 million to just half a million. The graph also shows how unemployment was 1.8 million in 1928 and peaked at 6 million in 1932 and that it fell to just 0.5 million in 1939.

Examiner's Comments on: Answer 1

1–2 out of 4

Unfortunately the candidate has made the common mistake of simply describing the source. He/she should have inferred what impact the Wall Street Crash (1929), Hitler's rise to power (January 1933) and rearmament had on unemployment levels in Germany. Sometimes it is impossible to make inferences unless background knowledge is applied to the source.

> **2** How useful is Source B as evidence about the success of the Nazi's economic policies?

Answer 2

Source B is an anti-Nazi propaganda poster by German communists. The poster suggests that the German economy only produced industrial goods in preparation for war. According to the poster German families are forced to eat bicycles, chains, nuts and bolts instead of essential food items like butter. The poster is clearly an exaggerated interpretation of what was going on in Germany. Preparation for war was seen as more important than providing luxury goods or even basic foodstuffs. Goering himself asked, 'Would you rather have butter or guns?' – he thereby admitted the Nazis' priority. The poster aimed to mock the Nazis' claim to have saved the German economy by pointing out that ordinary lives had not improved very much at all. Therefore the source tells us little about the actual success of Nazi policies but does present the interpretation of one of the Nazis' enemies.

Examiner's Comments on: Answer 2

3 out of 3

The candidate explores the nature, origin and purpose of the source to examine its usefulness. He/she clearly concludes the limited usefulness of this source as credible evidence.

> **3** Using Sources A and B and your own knowledge explain whether the Nazis improved the German economy.

Answer 3

Although Source A suggests that the Nazis miraculously wiped out unemployment, it fails to explore how this was done. The statistics give us a simplistic source of information and ignore the fact that millions of jobs were 'created' by sacking women, Jews and other minorities. Moreover thousands more were conscripted into the army and were therefore removed from unemployment figures. Hundreds of thousands were forced to work on public works schemes that, technically speaking, were paid jobs. In reality the work was hard, badly paid and conditions could be both squalid and dangerous. Also the world was generally recovering from the Great Depression and therefore the economy might have improved anyway.

Even though Source B is anti-Nazi propaganda, it correctly points out that the Nazis' economic policies were not designed to raise the Germans' standard of living. The economy was geared towards rearmament and German standards of living came second. The result was that by 1938 Germans were being paid less, for working longer than they were in 1928! Also the growing wealth of Germany was not being spent on higher wages or lower taxes, instead it was used to pay for new tanks, planes and machine-guns. Source B depicts an absurd German dinner but cleverly highlights the fact that whilst butter, cheese and coffee were in short supply Germany became the most powerful country in western Europe.

Examiner's Comments on: Answer 3

4 out of 5

Although the candidate dismisses any suggestion that the Nazis improved the German economy, the sources are combined well with extensive background knowledge to answer the question. However, this answer is too one-sided; the candidate should have briefly pointed out the genuine improvements in Germany's economy.

Practice Questions

1   What can you learn from the Source B about the Nazis' economic policies?
    HINT: What does the picture suggest about Nazi priorities?
2   How useful is Source A as evidence for the success of the Nazis' economic policies?
    HINT: Consider the nature of this source.
3   Using Sources A and B and your own knowledge explain how the Nazis drastically reduced unemployment in Germany between 1933 and 1939.

5. The world at war, 1938–45

Topic Summary

By 1945 up to 80 million people had been killed in the Second World War. German and Japanese aggression had sparked a war that most Europeans and Americans had hoped to avoid with policies like appeasement and isolationism. The initial German successes in Europe and those of Japan in the Far East eventually gave way to the combined military strength of the USA, the Soviet Union, Britain and their allies. The Allied victory in the summer of 1945 came about following five years of warfare that saw civilians as well as soldiers in the firing line.

What do I Need to Know?

You will need to assess the effectiveness of Appeasement in avoiding war. In addition you will need to be aware of German and Japanese successes in Europe and the Pacific, and ultimately why both countries had been defeated by 1945.

Key Events

30 September 1938
The **Munich Agreement**.

16 March 1939
Annexation of the rest of Czechoslovakia.

23 August 1939
The Nazi–Soviet Non-Aggression Pact.

1 September 1939
German invasion of Poland.

3 September 1939
British and French declaration of war.

9 April–22 June 1940
German defeat of Norway, Denmark, Holland, Belgium, Luxembourg and France.

10 July–September 1940
The **Battle of Britain**.

15 September 1940–41
The **Blitz**.

22 June 1941
Operation Barbarossa.

7 December 1941
The Japanese attack on Pearl Harbor.

18 May 1942
The Japanese complete their invasion of South East Asia.

4–5 June 1942
The Battle of Midway.

31 January 1943
Germany defeated at the Battle of Stalingrad.

14 March–22 June 1945
The Battle of Okinawa.

8 May 1945
German surrender, one week after Hitler's suicide.

6 August 1945
First atom bomb dropped on Hiroshima.

9 August 1945
Second atom bomb dropped on Nagasaki.

15 August 1945
Japanese surrender. The war is over.

Key Topics

What was the impact of Appeasement?

- Between 1938 and 1939 the British Prime Minister, Neville Chamberlain, believed that a war with Germany could be avoided if Britain (and France) were to give in to a number of Hitler's demands.

- Hitler's demands included the *Anschluss* (union) with Austria (March 1938) and the annexation of the Sudetenland (October 1938).

- In addition, Britain and France had ignored Germany's remilitarisation during the 1930s and had failed to punish Germany when the *Luftwaffe* had bombed the Spanish town of Guernica on 27 April 1937.

- This British and French foreign policy was called **Appeasement**. Its high point came at the Munich Conference in September 1938 when a German, British, French and Italian agreement transferred the Sudetenland from Czechoslovakia to German control.

- Appeasement failed to restrain Hitler and may have led to Hitler's ambitions actually growing.

- In March 1939 the Germans occupied the rest of Czechoslovakia. Hitler now demanded the Polish Corridor and the port of Danzig.

- The Nazi–Soviet Non-Aggression Pact agreed on 23 August 1939 enabled Germany to attack Poland without fearing an attack by the Soviet Union.

- The Nazi invasion of Poland on 1 September was followed two days later by a British and French declaration of war on Germany.

- Chamberlain had trusted Hitler's assurances that he had no more territorial ambitions after the Sudetenland. Hitler wrongly believed that Chamberlain would avoid war at all costs. Hitler was said to have been amazed when Britain actually declared war!

- Some historians have therefore argued that because of Appeasement, Britain failed to take the threat of Germany seriously until it was too late.

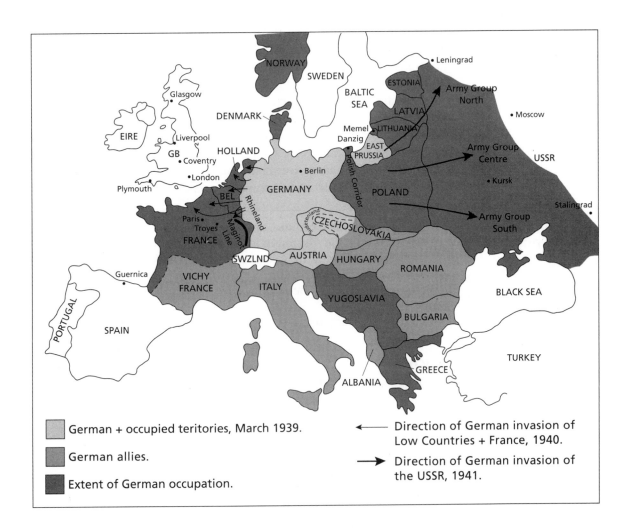

German + occupied teritories, March 1939.

German allies.

Extent of German occupation.

⟵—— Direction of German invasion of Low Countries + France, 1940.

——⟶ Direction of German invasion of the USSR, 1941.

Why were the Germans so successful in western Europe?

- The speed and size of the German army allowed a rapid victory that had been impossible in the First World War.
- **Blitzkrieg** enabled a combination of Stuka dive-bombers, highly trained paratroopers, fast Panzer tanks and well equipped and speedily supplied troops to conquer western Europe in the space of a few months.
- The collapse of Polish resistance had been achieved in less than a month. Between April and June 1940, Denmark, Belgium, Luxembourg, the Netherlands and France all fell to the Germans, whilst most of Norway and Sweden were occupied.

- The French had underestimated the strength and direction of a German attack. The well-fortified **Maginot Line** would have slowed down a German attack had the Germans attacked across it! Instead the Germans took the Allies by surprise and attacked through Belgium. They went round the Maginot Line and attacked France from the north.
- Unlike the First World War, those countries attacked by Germany were not prepared to fight what appeared to be a far superior enemy. In most cases they gave up rather than suffer in another world war.
- The French in particular surrendered very quickly. The ineffectiveness of the Maginot Line greatly damaged the morale of the French army, which then became defeatist.
- However, the Germans were well prepared for war and possessed a large professional army. Germany had more army divisions and trained soldiers than all of her western enemies combined.

What do I Know?

1 In what ways was Germany appeased before 1939?
2 Which country did Germany make a pact with in 1939?
3 Which military tactic helped the Germans make swift victories in 1939 and 1940?
4 Which countries had been conquered by the Germans by June 1940?
5 Which French defensive system failed to halt the German attack?

My score ....

Key Topic

The fall of France

- The rapid German advance caused panic throughout France.
- 5 million French people fled their homes and towns seeking a new home in the south. The population of Troyes fell from nearly 60,000 to just 30 in the summer of 1940!
- On 22 June 1940 France surrendered and was immediately split in two.
- German forces occupied northern and western France. The south and east were allowed to form a semi-autonomous state, known as **Vichy France**, which was governed by Marshal Pétain.
- Most occupied peoples, including the French, peacefully accepted German rule and hoped to survive the war.
- Small minority groups actively resisted German rule in the form of partisans; others collaborated with the Germans.

The survival of Britain

- 'Operation Sealion' was Hitler's plan to invade Britain across the English Channel. However, the plan was dependent on destroying the Royal Air Force.

- Between July and August 1940 the *Luftwaffe* unsuccessfully fought the RAF in the skies above the fields of southern England. *Spitfires* and *Hurricanes* were gradually able to shoot down German bombers. This period of the war became known as the 'Battle of Britain'.
- From September 1940 onwards, the *Luftwaffe* dropped its bombs on British cities in an attempt to destroy British morale. The Blitz, as it became known, was endured by the British people. The threat of an invasion passed and Hitler turned his attention to war against the Soviet Union.
- By November 1940 only Coventry and London had been bombed. However, in 1941 the *Luftwaffe* began bombing western ports in Plymouth, Liverpool and Glasgow in an attempt to disrupt the import of US supplies.

Operation Barbarossa and the war in the East

- Germany attacked the Soviet Union in June 1941 in **Operation Barbarossa**. They caught the Red Army completely by surprise.
- Blitzkrieg tactics enabled the Nazis to make huge advances of 50 miles (80 km) per day until late September 1941.
- Hitler ordered a daring three-pronged attack on the Soviet Union. The first prong headed north to Leningrad, the second headed east to Moscow, whilst the third aimed to head south-east to occupy the oil reserves of the Caucasus region.
- By the winter of 1941 Leningrad was virtually surrounded, the skyline of Moscow was in sight and Stalingrad was within reach. Stalin himself even ordered his private train to prepare for his escape to Siberia.
- 1941 was the Soviet Union's wettest autumn and coldest winter on record. The German advance became slowed and bogged down in the mud and was then literally frozen in by the severe winter.
- In 1942 the tide turned against the German army. This started with their defeat at the Battle of Stalingrad and the successful defence of Moscow.
- The Battle of Kursk in 1943 ended any hopes the Germans had of conquering the Soviet Union and turned the conflict into a defensive war for Germany.

What do I Know?

1 Who ruled Vichy France?
2 Which battle forced Hitler to abandon 'Operation Sealion'?
3 Why did the *Luftwaffe* bomb British cities?
4 What was 'Operation Barbarossa'?
5 What were the three targets of the German attack on the Soviet Union?
6 What helped to slow down the advance of the German army?

My score ....

Key Topic

Why were the Germans defeated?

- Hitler believed the German master race was destined to dominate Europe. This led him to make over-ambitious plans that resulted in Germany's eventual defeat.
- The rapid defeat of Poland and western Europe in 1939–40 encouraged Hitler still further and led to his daring plans to attack the Soviet Union.
- These quick successes in the West led Hitler to underestimate the determination of the British and Soviet people to defeat the German threat.
- The attack on the Soviet Union spread German forces too thinly whilst her soldiers were not prepared for the terrible Soviet winters.
- German supply lines became overstretched whilst her soldiers struggled to fight battles in the Soviet Union, the Balkans, Italy, North Africa, western Europe, Norway and in the Atlantic Ocean.
- Hitler attacked the Soviet Union in the East before he had destroyed the threat from Britain in the West.
- In December 1941 Hitler decided to declare war on the USA.
- From 1942 onwards, US and Allied attacks drew German troops away from the war against the Soviet Union and into Italy and France, particularly after the D-Day landings of June 1944.
- By late 1943 the Germans had become outnumbered and were unable to supply their army with sufficient munitions and weapons following the continuous air raids by US and British bombers.

Summary Box 1

The outbreak of war in the Pacific

- Following the Wall Street Crash and the Great Depression, the Japanese army (which was devoted to its Emperor, **Hirohito**) had controlled the Japanese government.
- Throughout the 1930s and 40s the Japanese army believed that the creation of an empire would solve their economic problems.
- Manchuria (1931), China (1937) and large areas of eastern Asia were attacked and occupied as the Japanese created their 'Greater East Asia Co-Prosperity Sphere'.

- These areas were intended to supply Japan with all the raw materials its economy needed, particularly the oil fields in South East Asia.
- Only the size of the US army and navy threatened to curb Japanese expansion. However, Japan's biggest problem was that it relied on the USA for 80 per cent of the oil it needed for factories and fuel.
- When the USA banned the export of oil to Japan in July 1941 the Japanese government was faced with a clear decision; either withdraw from its positions in China and Indo-China or declare war on the USA.
- On 7 December 1941 Japanese bombers attacked the US navy's main Pacific base at Pearl Harbor. 21 American warships and 300 planes were either destroyed or damaged, whilst 2300 Americans died. The Japanese lost just 29 out of 360 planes in the attack.
- On 8 December 1941 the USA and Britain declared war on Japan.

What do I Know?

1 Which two countries successfully countered German attacks?
2 Where were German forces fighting during the Second World War?
3 What mistakes did Hitler make during the Second World War?
4 Why did Japan wish to build an empire?
5 When did the Allies declare war on Japan?

My score ....

Key Topic

Why were the Japanese defeated?

- The Japanese government believed that the only way to beat the USA was to inflict a surprise attack on the US navy.
- Whilst the attack on Pearl Harbor came as a surprise, it failed to destroy the heart of the US navy. Planes and warships were quickly replaced, whilst oil reserves and the all-important aircraft carriers were completely unaffected.
- Following the Battle of Midway on 4 June 1942, the US navy completely controlled the Pacific.
- Victory would eventually be achieved through a process of 'island hopping' in order to re-capture the islands the Japanese had captured, and then 'leapfrogging' towards Japan itself. This process was to inflict enormous casualties on both sides.
- Between March and June 1945 the Japanese demonstrated the determination with which they would continue to fight the war, despite a victory appearing increasingly impossible. At the Battle of Okinawa the Japanese lost 240,000 lives, 8000 aircraft and one battleship – in the defence of one island.

- Nearly 40,000 US casualties and the loss of 800 US aircraft on Okinawa demonstrated to US **President Truman** that the war against Japan might last years and result in massive Allied casualties. This influenced his decision to authorise the dropping of atomic bombs on the Japanese towns of Hiroshima and Nagasaki on 6 and 9 August 1945.
- A combination of the Soviet Union's declaration of war (9 August), the continual air raids on Japanese cities, an increasingly starving population and the devastation of atomic bombs led the Japanese government to surrender.
- On 15 August 1945 Emperor Hirohito officially surrendered on Japanese public radio. The Second World War had ended.

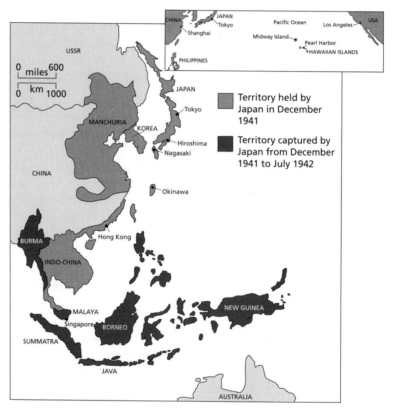

▲ **Map of Asia showing Japanese advances.**

What do I Know?

1 Why was the Japanese attack on Pearl Harbor not a disaster for the USA?

2 Which naval battle was a turning point in the war in the Pacific?

3 How did the capture of Okinawa affect the USA's military strategy?

4 Which Japanese cities suffered an atomic attack in August 1945?

5 Why did the Japanese government decide to surrender?

My score ....

Key Words and Names

Appeasement
British and French foreign policy between 1936 and 1939.

The Blitz
Bombing of major British cities by the *Luftwaffe* in an attempt to destroy British morale and disrupt the war effort.

Blitzkrieg
German 'Lightning War' involving modern technology aimed at securing rapid victories.

Battle of Britain
Aerial battles between the RAF and the *Luftwaffe* to gain control over Britain's skies. Ended in September 1940 when the *Luftwaffe* began the Blitz.

Emperor Hirohito
Japanese head of state during the Second World War.

Maginot Line
Strong defences along the French border with Germany and Luxembourg.

Munich Agreement
Agreement signed by Germany, Britain, France and Italy that gave the Sudetenland to Germany in September 1939.

Operation Barbarossa
Name given to the German attack on the Soviet Union on 22 June 1941.

Vichy France
The semi-autonomous French state created by the Nazis and led by Marshal Pétain.

President Truman
US President following Roosevelt's death in April 1945.

Exam Type Questions

Study the sources and questions carefully. Attempt the questions yourself, then compare your answers with the answers given and check the examiner's comments.

Source A

The Japanese and US government headed towards an inevitable showdown throughout 1941. The central issue was over oil and Japan's growing need for a cheap supply. Japan had two possible options: firstly, it could continue buying expensive imports from the USA. Secondly, it could create an empire in south east Asia and get oil for free. The Japanese felt the issue of oil was becoming a tool used by the Americans to dictate their foreign policy.

▲ **An extract from a modern textbook.**

Source B

▲ **A photograph of the destruction caused at Pearl Harbor.**

> **1** What can you learn from Source A about why the Japanese
> attacked Pearl Harbor?

Answer 1

This source suggests that the Japanese believed they had no option other than to create an empire so they could gain a cheap supply of oil. Source A implies that the Japanese felt blackmailed by the Americans, who might cut off oil supplies unless they did as they were told. Therefore the Japanese attack on Pearl Harbor was an attempt to prevent the USA interfering in their creation of an empire in South East Asia.

Examiner's Comments on: Answer 1

4 out of 4

The candidate picks out the key inferences and concludes that the Japanese felt an attack was their only option.

> **2** How useful is Source B as evidence about the success of the Japanese attack on Pearl Harbor.

Answer 2

The photograph gives the impression of utter destruction and chaos as the US navy struggles to fight raging fires and sinking battleships. This is in one sense an accurate portrayal since four US battleships were sunk and another 17 were badly damaged. In addition 2300 Americans lost their lives. The US government probably used this photograph for propaganda purposes. It would easily generate a desire for revenge and war amongst previously isolationist Americans. In fact the photograph only captures one aspect of the Japanese attack on Pearl Harbor and cannot possibly show how the attack failed to destroy oil reserves, the modern US warships or the four crucial aircraft carriers that were safely out at sea.

Examiner's Comments on: Answer 2

3 out of 3

The candidate explores the nature and purpose of the source very carefully. The source is not dismissed as entirely useless but its limitations are analysed by applying sound background knowledge.

> **3** Using Sources A and B and your own knowledge explain why the USA declared war on Japan.

Answer 3

Source A suggests that the USA feared the impact of a Japanese empire in Asia. The USA enjoyed enormous economic prosperity and free trade in this region and knew that a Japanese empire would restrict this. The source implies that the Japanese were determined to rival US power and dominance and were prepared to use war to do this. In contrast Source B suggests that that the USA's declaration of war was motivated by a desire for revenge

> against the cruel attack on Pearl Harbor. This may have been the reason why the US people supported the war. However the US government was probably more worried about the consequences of a Japanese empire in the East and a Nazi empire in the West on their trade links and the economy.

Examiner's Comments on: Answer 3

5 out of 5

The candidate uses the sources effectively to begin gathering reasons. Background knowledge is then applied to give a clear answer to the question.

Practice Questions

1   What can you learn from Source B about the Japanese attack on Pearl Harbor in 1941?

2   How useful is Source A as evidence about why the Japanese and US governments went to war against each other in 1941?
HINT: Consider the nature and purpose of this source.

3   Using Sources A and B and your own knowledge explain whether the Japanese air attack on Pearl Harbor was successful or not.
HINT: Compare what Source B *suggests* against what you know.

6. Conflict in Vietnam, c.1963–75

Topic Summary

Between 1945 and 1964 the USA became increasingly involved in the defence of South Vietnam against communists rebels. When open warfare broke out in 1964 the USA was drawn into a conflict that lasted a further 9 years and drained the US of lives, wealth and prestige around the world. The basis of the USA's involvement was the fear that the very future of freedom was at stake, yet it became a war that most Americans finally opposed and have since grown to regret. The atrocities committed on both sides and the enormous civilian casualties have made the conflict in Vietnam a symbol of the horror and futility of war.

What do I Need to Know?

You will need to be aware of how and why the USA's involvement in Vietnam developed between 1945 and 1964. In addition you will need to compare the tactics used by Presidents Johnson and Nixon. Finally you must understand why the USA withdrew from Vietnam in 1973 and what impact the war had on both sides.

Key Events

1954
Following a conference in Geneva the French colony of Indo-China is split into three new countries; Laos, Cambodia and Vietnam. Vietnam is then temporarily split in two (North and South) pending elections in 1956.

January–May 1961
President Kennedy sends 16,000 advisers to assist the South Vietnamese Army (**ARVN**).

August 1964
The Gulf of Tonkin incident.

February 1965
The start of 'Operation Rolling Thunder'. This lasts until mid-1968.

January 1968
The Tet Offensive.

January 1973
The USA and North Vietnam agree to a ceasefire. The USA agrees to withdraw its troops and hold free elections to let South Vietnamese people decide the future of their country.

March 1974
The last US soldier is withdrawn from Vietnam.

April 30 1975
The **Vietcong** finally capture South Vietnam.
1976
North and South Vietnam are unified. The capital, Saigon, is renamed Ho Chi Minh City.

Key Topics

How did the USA become involved in a war in Vietnam?

Stage One: 1945–52

- In this period President Truman sent $3 billion worth of aid to the French army who were struggling to retain control of their **colony** called 'Indo-China' of which Vietnam formed a part. The French were forced to retreat against communist rebels led by **Ho Chi Minh**.

Stage Two: 1952–4

- Under Eisenhower the USA funded 80 per cent of the French war effort against the communist rebels. The money was wasted because the French were on the verge of being defeated by the well organised communists.

Stage Three: 1954–62

- Following a conference in Geneva, the French agreed to withdraw from Indo-China. The colony was then split into three new countries; Cambodia, Laos and Vietnam.
- Initially Vietnam was split into North and South, with the hope that the country would unify following free elections planned for 1956.
- Ho Chi Minh, a communist dictator, led North Vietnam. He received financial and military aid from both China and the USSR.
- South Vietnam was ruled by **Ngo Dinh Diem**; a corrupt right-wing dictator. Ngo Dinh Diem's government received a further $1 billion of aid from the USA. The USA hoped he would defend South Vietnam from any communist attacks from North Vietnam.

Stage Four: 1963–4

- Between 1958 and 1962 the South Vietnamese Army (ARVN), had come under increasing attacks from communist guerrillas who called themselves the National Liberation Front (NLF). The NLF were called the Vietcong by the USA.
- **President Kennedy** hoped to counter this communist threat when he sent 16,000 advisers to South Vietnam in 1963. These advisers trained the ARVN in **guerrilla warfare** and were the first US troops to land on Vietnamese soil.

- The ARVN were unable to cope with the threat of communist guerrillas and relied on US support.
- The USA had to decide whether to let South Vietnam fall to communism or send in troops to destroy the communist threat once and for all.

Stage Five: 1964–8

- Following two attacks on the US naval ship *USS Maddox* in the Gulf of Tonkin by North Vietnamese gunboats, the US Congress gave **President Johnson** virtually unlimited powers to eliminate the communist threat.
- From 1964 onwards the USA's involvement in Vietnam escalated year on year. By 1965 the USA had begun **air raids** on suspected Vietcong targets. This tactic was called 'Operation Rolling Thunder'. In addition the USA began sending more and more troops into Vietnam.
- By the end of 1968 well over half a million US troops were in Vietnam, 30,000 had died and the war was costing the USA $30 billion per year.

Stage Six: 1968–75

- Following the Tet Offensive in January 1968 the USA began peace talks with North Vietnam. A ceasefire was not reached for another 5 years.
- At the same time **President Nixon** introduced his **Vietnamisation** policy. Nixon hoped to 'bring the boys back home' by forcing the ARVN to take greater responsibility for fighting the Vietcong.
- Despite calling for peace talks, Nixon increased air raids on Vietcong targets and supply lines. This included attacks on neutral Cambodia and Laos.
- By mid-1973 open war had again broken out between the Vietcong and the ARVN. The USA finally stood back and accepted the communist takeover of South Vietnam.
- In April 1975 Saigon was captured and South Vietnam joined with North Vietnam the following year.

What do I Know?

1 When did the state of Vietnam come into existence?
2 Who were the leaders of North and South Vietnam?
3 What were the names of the two armies of North and South Vietnam?
4 Which event sparked full US involvement in Vietnam?
5 Which event in 1968 sparked a shift in US policy in Vietnam?

My score ....

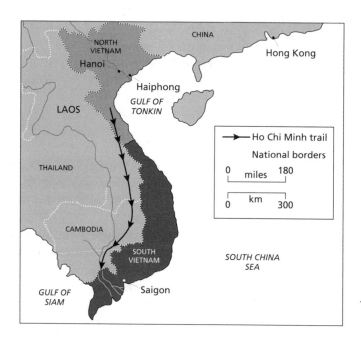

◀ **The division of Vietnam.**

Key Topic

Why did the USA get involved in the war in Vietnam?

- After the Second World War the USA feared the expansion of communism across Europe and Asia. The USA believed that the future of US prosperity and democracy was at risk if communism were allowed to spread.
- By 1956 the Soviet Union, China, eastern Europe and North Korea all had communist governments. Americans felt increasingly threatened by the spread of communism.
- US politicians feared that if another country became communist they could 'infect' neighbouring states.
- This fear was based on the **Domino Theory** and meant that if, for example, South Vietnam was 'allowed to go communist' then other Asian nations would become communist as well. US politicians believed the fall of South Vietnam would be soon followed by Laos, Cambodia, Thailand, Burma, India and Pakistan.

What was the nature of the war in Vietnam?

- Vietnam was an agricultural nation with few large towns or cities. Most people lived in the countryside surrounded by dense forests, and worked in the paddy fields.
- Vietnam's terrain meant that a war would be unlike anything the US army had ever experienced before. Traditional battles involving tanks, dive-bombers and enormous infantry attacks would be impossible.
- The Vietcong dug thousands of kilometres of tunnels, from which they launched surprise attacks on isolated US or ARVN units. After an attack they quickly disappeared into their network of tunnels or hid among sympathetic Vietnamese peasants.

US tactics

- The initial US response was called 'Operation Rolling Thunder' and lasted from February 1965 until mid 1968. This involved the continuous **carpet bombing** of enemy towns, factories, railways and bases. In an attempt to prevent supplies arriving from North Vietnam to the Vietcong, the US Air Force bombed the **Ho Chi Minh Trail** in neutral Laos and Cambodia.

- These bombing missions killed innocent Vietnamese civilians and led to increased hatred of the USA. One US officer said, after the town of Ben-Tre was destroyed, 'it became necessary to destroy the town in order to save it.'

- Three times as many explosives were dropped on Vietnam than throughout the entire Second World War.

- In an attempt to destroy the Vietcong in their secret forest hideouts, a quarter of Vietnam's forests were destroyed from the air with **Agent Orange** and **napalm**.

- US ground forces attempted to tackle the Vietcong through **search and destroy missions** which tried to locate and eliminate Vietcong soldiers. They found this very difficult because the Vietcong either hid in their tunnels or merged with ordinary peasants.

- Both sides broke the **Geneva Convention** and caused Vietnamese people to live in fear of attacks from the Vietcong, US army and the ARVN.

- Both sides committed atrocities against innocent civilians. In March 1968 in the village of My Lai, for example, over 500 innocent Vietnamese men, women and children were murdered by US troops.

Vietcong tactics

- US soldiers lived in constant fear of surprise attacks, booby traps and Vietcong guerrillas dressed as ordinary Vietnamese peasants.

- However, the Vietcong did not rely on guerrilla tactics alone. On 30 January 1968 the Vietcong launched simultaneous attacks on numerous South Vietnamese towns and bases using conventional battle tactics. This Tet Offensive caught the US government and people by surprise.

- Despite the eventual failure of the Tet Offensive (80,000 Vietcong killed), the attack brought about a shift in the opinion of the US public and President Johnson himself.

- Johnson immediately ended air bombings and sought peace talks with the Vietcong. At the same time he declared that he would not attempt to be re-elected as president.

What do I Know?

1 What theory was the basis of the USA's involvement in Vietnam?
2 What type of warfare did the Vietcong use?
3 How did the US armed forces attempt to destroy the Vietcong?
4 Which convention did both sides break?
5 Which event brought about a shift in President Johnson's policy in Vietnam?

My score ....

Key Topic

What was the impact of the war?

A) *The impact on US foreign policy*

- Presidents Johnson and Nixon were criticised for what many saw as an abuse of their power.
- Nixon in particular was accused of lying to Congress over the precise nature of the US Air Force's bombing missions over the Ho Chi Minh Trail.
- The result was that Congress passed the War Powers Act in 1973. This greatly limited a president's power to conduct a war abroad.
- The war in Vietnam made the USA far more reluctant to become involved in future conflicts.
- The US public, which had grown suspicious of any involvement of US troops abroad, encouraged this new attitude.
- Between 1973 and the fall of communism in Europe in the 1990s, the USA preferred to fight communism by funding anti-communist rebels and leaders in places like Afghanistan, El Salvador, the Philippines, Nicaragua and Angola.
- It was not until the Gulf War in 1991 that the USA fought in another major foreign war.

B) *The impact on US soldiers*

- Most of the 9 million soldiers who fought in Vietnam were **drafted** into the army. Their average age was just 19.
- High School students were occasionally drafted on the basis of the grades and attendance records they had achieved in their final year of High School. High School teachers were known to give their students straight A's rather than allow them to be conscripted.
- Thousands of US youths joined hippie communes, escaped to Canada or studied in Europe rather than face the draft. These young Americans were labelled 'draft dodgers' by their fellow citizens.
- An average 'tour of duty' lasted one year.
- The majority of conscripts were from **blue-collar** backgrounds. A disproportionate number of minority groups were drafted into the

army; African Americans were twice as likely as white Americans to be drafted, whilst Hispanics were three times as likely.

- The constant fear of Vietcong attack took its toll on US soldiers. Half turned to cannabis, whilst one-fifth became addicted to heroin.
- Of the 8,744,000 soldiers who served in Vietnam, 58,000 died, 150,000 were wounded, half a million deserted whilst 700,000 required psychological counselling after the war.
- Vietnam veterans struggled to return to ordinary civilian life and became more likely to be involved in crime, drug addiction or commit suicide.
- When US soldiers returned from Vietnam they were denied a heroes' welcome and were often condemned by fellow Americans who considered their actions immoral.
- Vietnam veterans were often confused by the fact they had followed orders on their tour of duty, yet suffered insults and shame when they returned home.

C) The impact on US civilians

- At first the US people fully backed US involvement in Vietnam.
- By 1968 the majority of Americans opposed the war for a number of reasons:
  - The Tet Offensive suddenly made Americans realise that the war in Vietnam was not going to be easy to win.
  - Newspapers and television cameras recorded atrocities committed by US soldiers, for example, the My Lai massacre.
  - Nightly television reports demonstrated horrific war crimes committed by ARVN soldiers. For example, in 1968, footage showed a Vietcong soldier being shot point blank in the head by an ARVN soldier.
  - The cost of the war ($141 billion) had destroyed President Johnson's 'Great Society' programme and weakened the US economy (see page 130).
  - Anti-war protesters included influential voices in music (Bob Dylan), sport (Mohammed Ali) and politics (Martin Luther King).

D) The impact on Vietnamese people

- US bombers and ground attacks led to approximately 2.5 million Vietnamese deaths. The cities of Hanoi and Haiphong were virtually flattened by US bombers. However, this only made the communists even more determined to win.
- North Vietnamese people were also drafted and ordered to serve in Vietcong units in South Vietnam.
- Millions of innocent South Vietnamese peasants were terrorised and bombed by both sides.
- Vietnam had grown enough food to feed its own people, but warfare led to starvation and hunger throughout Vietnam.
- 50,000 'American Asian' children were born to Vietnamese women and US soldiers.

- Vietnam itself was environmentally devastated. One-quarter of its forests were destroyed, and chemicals like Agent Orange and napalm caused long term damage to the region's food chain and ecological systems. Vietnam's once vibrant rice export trade was ruined.
- Following the war, violent reprisals against alleged American sympathisers and allies in Vietnam led to over 1 million Vietnamese refugees or 'boat people'.

Summary Box 1

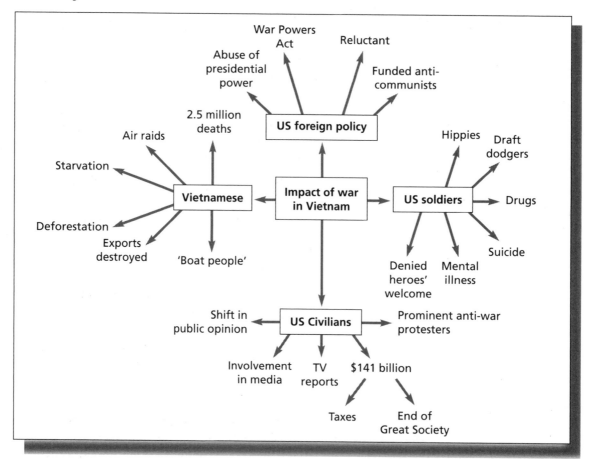

War Powers Act

Abuse of presidential power

Reluctant

Funded anti-communists

US foreign policy

2.5 million deaths

Air raids

Starvation

Vietnamese

Impact of war in Vietnam

US soldiers

Hippies

Draft dodgers

Drugs

Deforestation

Exports destroyed

'Boat people'

Denied heroes' welcome

Mental illness

Suicide

Shift in public opinion

US Civilians

Prominent anti-war protesters

Involvement in media

TV reports

$141 billion

Taxes

End of Great Society

What do I Know?

1 Which new law limited the powers of the US president?
2 How did the US army recruit new soldiers?
3 What name was given to Americans who successfully avoided conscription?
4 How long did a US soldier spend in Vietnam?
5 What were the casualty figures during the Vietnam War?
6 Which attack affected US public opinion?
7 In which Vietnamese village did US soldiers carry out a massacre?
8 How much did the war in Vietnam cost the USA?
9 Which Vietnamese cities were destroyed by US air raids?
10 Which chemicals damaged Vietnam's natural environment?

My score ....

Why did the USA lose the war in Vietnam?

- The USA never managed to win the support of ordinary Vietnamese people because:
  - They were always seen as a foreign occupying force.
  - Ho Chi Minh was a national hero after the Second World War.
  - Ho Chi Minh redistributed land among the peasants and awarded greater rights to women.
  - The USA allied herself with the hated and corrupt government of South Vietnam.
  - The USA's allies, the ARVN, were despised by ordinary peasants because of their corrupt and brutal activities.
  - US soldiers committed atrocities of their own.
  - The US army was unable to defeat the guerrilla tactics of the Vietcong, whose soldiers were more determined and knew the terrain well.
  - Aerial bombings failed to destroy the Vietcong, and instead led to increased civilian casualties and hatred towards the Americans.
- Nixon's policy of Vietnamisation failed to stop the advance of the Vietcong. The ARVN lacked leadership, morale and support.

What happened to Vietnam?

- By 1975 the US had withdrawn all military and economic support to Vietnam.
- The Vietcong defeated the ARVN and destroyed all opposition. Saigon in South Vietnam was captured in 1975 and renamed Ho Chi Minh City.
- In 1976 North and South Vietnam were officially reunited under a communist government.
- Burma, India, Thailand, Pakistan and Malaysia did not fall to the communists, despite the Domino Theory fears. In fact, after 1976, communist Vietnam became involved in wars with both communist Cambodia and communist China.

What do I Know?

1 Why was Ho Chi Minh popular among Vietnamese people?
2 Why did Vietnamese people dislike the ARVN?
3 Which policy did Nixon hope would allow the withdrawal of US soldiers from Vietnam?
4 What name was Saigon given after it was captured?
5 When were North and South Vietnam reunited?

My score ....

**Key Words
and Names**

Agent Orange
A toxic chemical with the ability to defoliate or burn away undergrowth, weeds and leaves. It was supposed to expose Vietcong positions. It later caused cancer among Vietnamese people and US troops.

Air raids
Explosive bombs dropped by fighter planes.

ARVN
The South Vietnamese army.

Blue collar
US term used to describe the working classes.

Carpet bombing
Enormous airborne attacks on enemy targets.

Colony
An area of land under the control of another country.

Domino Theory
An American view that the triumph of communism in one country might lead to the spread of communism in neighbouring countries.

Drafted
Compulsory conscription into the army.

Geneva Convention
A series of agreements since 1864 between all major nations. The various conventions agreed on the rules of warfare and the treatment of prisoners and civilians. Violation of the convention was intended to lead to war crime tribunals.

Guerrilla warfare
Unconventional fighting tactics where small groups of soldiers take on the enemy in surprise isolated attacks before quickly retreating and selecting another enemy target.

Ho Chi Minh
Communist leader of North Vietnam and later the whole of Vietnam.

Ho Chi Minh Trail
The Vietcong's supply lines that ran from North Vietnam through Cambodia and Laos into South Vietnam.

Napalm
A highly inflammable and inextinguishable liquid sprayed over Vietcong bases, soldiers and civilians.

Search and destroy missions
US army's unsuccessful strategy to try and hunt down the Vietcong by entering dense forests searching for enemy hideouts and bases.

Vietcong
American name given to the 'National Liberation Front' (NLF). The NLF were South Vietnamese communist rebels, led and backed by North Vietnam.

Vietnamisation
President Nixon's attempt to withdraw US troops from Vietnam by providing massive military aid to the ARVN as they retreated.

Ngo Dinh Diem
American-backed leader of South Vietnam, assassinated in November 1963.

President Kennedy
Sent 16,000 advisers to support the ARVN's defence against Vietcong guerrillas.

President Johnson
Chiefly responsible for escalating the war against the Vietcong and initiating massive US involvement.

President Nixon
Became popular in the USA for his policy of Vietnamisation that allowed US troops to leave Vietnam. He also increased air raids on Vietcong targets.

Exam Type Questions

Study the sources and questions carefully. Attempt the questions yourself, then compare your answers with the answers given and check the examiner's comments.

Source A

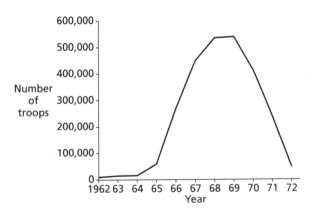

▲ The number of US troops in Vietnam between 1962 and 1972.

Source B

It was explained to us that anything alive in that area was supposed to be dead. We were told that if we saw a 'gook' [slang for Vietnamese] or thought we saw one, no matter how big or small, shoot first. No need for permission to fire. It was just an 'open turkey shoot' … men, women and children, no matter what their ages all went into the body count. This operation went on for a few weeks. This was a regular 'search and destroy' mission in which we destroyed everything we found.

▲ An account of US battle tactics from Sergeant James Weeks in May 1967.

> **1** What can you learn from Source A about the level of US involvement in Vietnam in the 1960s and 70s?

Answer 1

This source suggests that US involvement in Vietnam escalated throughout the 1960s and peaked in 1968-9, before a rapid decrease in troop numbers occurred. The sudden increase after 1964 reflects the escalation by Johnson after the Gulf of Tonkin incident in August 1964. Similarly the decrease in troop numbers under Nixon (1969-74) reflects his policy of 'Vietnamisation' that basically replaced US troops with increased air raids.

Examiner's Comments on: Answer 1

3 out of 4

The candidate uses his/her knowledge to comprehend the history behind the figures. The source is placed in its historical context and the candidate is therefore able to show how the troop numbers illustrate stages in the Vietnam conflict.

> **2** How useful is Source B as evidence about the tactics used by the US army in Vietnam?

Answer 2

The source is useful because we are informed that soldiers were told to shoot on sight, even if they killed lots of innocent people. The source shows that US troops acted illegally by killing unarmed civilians and illustrates their immoral tactics.

Examiner's Comments on: Answer 2

1 out of 3

The candidate examines the content of the source without considering its nature, origin or purpose. In the case of this source its origin is the most important feature. It comes from a sergeant in the US army who admits something that the US government officially denied took place. The fact it was admitted proves how desperate the US army had become and how useless 'search and destroy' missions were. This makes Source B very useful indeed.

> **3** Using Sources A and B and your own knowledge explain how the US involvement in Vietnam changed between 1963 and 1975.

Answer 3

Between 1963 and 1975 the US government moved through a series of very different levels of involvement in Vietnam. Source A shows how Kennedy sent 16,000 'advisers' to Vietnam to train the South Vietnamese Army (ARNV) in 1963. This was an attempt to counter the communist threat from North Vietnam.

However, President Johnson was convinced by the Domino Theory, which is why he personally authorised the escalation of US involvement after the Gulf of Tonkin incident in August 1964. As Source A shows, troop numbers rose from 60,000 to 535,000. This demonstrates Johnson's massive escalation of the USA's involvement in the war with his 'Operation Rolling Thunder' campaign that combined aerial bombing with thousands of attacks on Vietcong positions by US soldiers. It was during this period that the US army began to question the assumption that the Vietcong could be beaten. The Vietcong's guerrilla tactics successfully held back the US army who were then forced to use 'search and destroy' missions (Source B) that were to create so much hatred of the USA among the Vietnamese people.

Following the Tet Offensive in January 1968 and the growing anti-war public opinion across the USA, the US government decided to change tactics. Under Nixon (1969-74) troop numbers fell dramatically from 539,000 to 47,000. This highlights Nixon's hugely popular 'Vietnamisation' policy that armed ARNV troops instead of US troops and stepped up air raids on Vietcong targets.

By 1975 the Vietnamisation policy had failed and the USA had long since withdrawn all support for the ARNV who were unable to cope with the Vietcong advances.

Examiner's Comments on: Answer 3

5 out of 5

This candidate has a very good knowledge of the stages and levels of US involvement in Vietnam. He/she cleverly uses the sources to demonstrate these stages and provides explanations of why the USA changed its policies towards Vietnam.

7. The end of apartheid in South Africa, 1982–94

Topic Summary

When PW Botha became the South African President in 1978 he inherited a deeply segregated and unjust society. Botha introduced reforms which he hoped would guarantee the survival of the **apartheid** system, but instead led to chaos and divisions that pushed South Africa to the verge of a civil war. When FW De Klerk replaced Botha in 1989 he accepted that the National Party's control of South Africa was at an end and that greater freedom and democracy was the only direction for South Africa. **Nelson Mandela's** release in 1990 marked a new beginning for South Africa and led to the eventual dismantling of apartheid and the introduction of equal rights throughout South Africa.

What do I Need to Know?

You will need to know how successive South American prime ministers created the apartheid system and the impact this had on South Africans' lives. In addition you will need to understand why South Africa was in a state of crisis by the late 1980s and why De Klerk's National Party gave way to widespread protests and accepted the destruction of apartheid.

Key Events

1948
The National Party wins the general election and Dr Malan becomes Prime Minister.

1950–3
The National Party introduces a series of laws that lay the foundations of apartheid.

1959
Bantu Self-Government Act.

March 1960
The Sharpeville Massacre leads to formation of the MK ('Spear of the Nation').

June 1976
Soweto Uprising.

September 1977
Death of Steve Biko.

September 1978
Botha becomes Prime Minister.

1983
The United Democratic Front (UDF) is formed.

1984
Botha introduces the new South African Constitution.

1985
Botha declares a **state of emergency**.

August 1989
De Klerk takes over as President.

February 1990
Mandela is released and De Klerk promises equal rights for all South Africans.

April 1994
South Africa holds its first democratic elections. Mandela is elected South African President.

Key Topics

A background to South African history

- Southern Africa had been home to native Khoi, San, Bantu and Zulu tribes for hundreds of years.
- In the seventeenth century Dutch settlers arrived and in the nineteenth century British settlers arrived in South Africa.
- At the beginning of the twentieth century South Africa was a multi-cultural society.

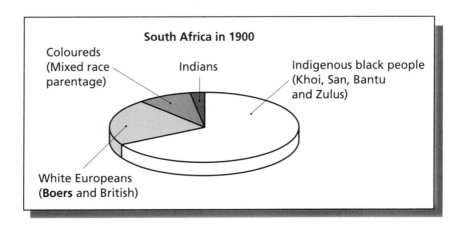

South Africa in 1900

- Even before the election of the National Party in 1948, non-white people were treated as second-class citizens:
  - Black people were forced into dangerous and low-paid jobs in the mines.
  - Black people were unable to choose the land on which they lived or farmed.
  - Black and white communities lived apart.
  - **Pass Laws** restricted the free movement of black people.
  - Black people were barred from the best-paid jobs.

What was the nature of the National Party's rule up to 1978?

- Support for the National Party came mainly from white South Africans of Dutch origin. These people were known as 'Boers' or 'Afrikaners'.
- When the National Party won the election in May 1948 by just five seats, it had already outlined the Party's plans for apartheid in the Sauer Report:
  - Blacks to live in special reserves.
  - Any blacks in white areas to be classed as 'temporary visitors'.
  - Indians to be sent back to India.
  - Only whites to have the right to vote.
- Apartheid was gradually expanded by Daniel Malan and his National Party successors for the next 40 years.

Daniel Malan, Prime Minister 1948–54

- Malan laid the foundations of apartheid by proposing laws that divided society and made non-whites second-class citizens.
  - 1949: **Prohibition of Mixed Marriages Act:**
    It became a crime for white and non-white people to marry one another and/or have children.
  - 1950: **Population Registration Act:**
    All South Africans were to be classified according to racial origin. Civil rights were then awarded according to their racial classification.
  - 1950: **Group Areas Act:**
    This divided all towns and cities into white and non-white districts. This ethnic cleansing forced the migration of 3.5 million people; only 70,000 of these were white.
  - 1952: **Abolition of Passes Act:**
    This Act extended compulsory passes amongst black men and women in all urban areas.
  - 1953: **Separate Amenities Act:**
    Public facilities like swimming pools and parks were segregated.
  - 1953: **Bantu Education Act:**
    All schools were placed under government control. Curricula were changed to reinforce the theory of white superiority. Government spending on a black pupil was just one-sixth of that spent on a white pupil.

Hendrik Verwoerd, Prime Minister 1958–66

- Verwoerd wanted:
  - an all-white South Africa by 1978.
  - the complete and permanent division of races in South Africa.
- Verwoerd was able to introduce even more radical changes because the National Party now controlled the South African police, courts, media, civil service, all levels of government and the army.

- **1959: Bantu Self-Government Act:**
  - ○ Verwoerd recommended the creation of eight (later ten) self-governing homelands for the various black peoples. These homelands were known as Bantustans.
  - ○ He hoped to 'cleanse' the rest of South Africa of non-whites and force them into these new homelands.
  - ○ Verwoerd planned to monitor the economy and government of these new homelands and prepare them for self-rule.
  - ○ Verwoerd was assassinated before his plans were achieved.

John Vorster, Prime Minister 1966–78

- Vorster hoped to complete Verwoerd's vision of Bantustans across South Africa.
  - ○ Between 1976 and 1981 four Bantustans were created (Transkei, Bophuthatswana, Venda and Ciskei). They were too overcrowded and financially weak to stand any chance of prosperity.
  - ○ Each Bantustan had its own leader. These leaders were all approved by the National Party and were little more than '**puppet leaders**'.
  - ○ In theory, movement in and out of Bantustans was banned. In practice, millions of blacks survived by illegally commuting into white districts.

What do I Know?

1 To what extent was South Africa a multi-cultural society by 1900?
2 Who were the main supporters of the National Party?
3 What plans did the National Party have for South Africa in 1948?
4 How did Daniel Malan lay the foundations of apartheid during the 1940s and 50s?
5 Describe how the National Party was able to control South Africa so effectively.
6 Name the four Bantustans set up between 1976 and 1981.
7 Why did Verwoerd and Vorster wish to introduce Bantustans across South Africa?

My score ....

Key Topic

Who opposed apartheid in South Africa?

The African National Congress (ANC)

- Formed in 1923, originally by a middle-class group of black South Africans.

- **Nelson Mandela** and **Walter Sisulu** joined the ANC in 1943 but felt the organisation lacked the determination and radicalism needed to improve the lives of black people.
- By 1948 Mandela and Sisulu were elected to the governing body of the ANC and set about making the organisation far more effective.
- In 1952 the ANC called on all black people to ignore segregation laws and be involved in non-violent protest. Thousands were arrested and the world media became aware of the injustices in South Africa. Membership of the ANC rocketed from 10,000 to 100,000 in the space of months.
- In 1955 the ANC organised a rally and declared the 'Freedom Charter'; a list of demands for basic civil rights. The crowd contained thousands of blacks, coloureds, Indians and whites.
- The Sharpeville Massacre (see page 83) convinced Mandela and most other ANC members that non-violent protests were proving useless. As a result the Umkhonto we Sizwe (MK), meaning 'Spear of the Nation', was formed. This organisation targeted power stations, electricity pylons and other key economic targets in South Africa with homemade explosives.
- Prominent ANC leaders, like Mandela, went into hiding. However, in 1962 **BOSS**, the secret police, tracked Mandela down and put him in prison. The following year all the other MK leaders were captured in their hideout at Rivonia. In 1964 all were sentenced to life imprisonment on Robben Island.
- Support for the ANC lost its momentum after 1964; it seemed that they had been defeated. It was not until the mid 1970s that the ANC once more threatened the apartheid system.

Black consciousness

- From the mid 1960s to mid 1970s opposition to apartheid took the form of raising black pride and consciousness.
- The movement encouraged the study of African history, languages and culture. It aimed to maintain self respect and pride amongst black South Africans in spite of the apartheid system.
- The most famous exponent of this movement was a medical student called Stephen Biko who set up the South African Students' Organisation (SASO). His ideas inspired the **Soweto Schools Uprising**; this led to Biko's imprisonment and eventual death in police custody.
- The Soweto Schools Uprising in June 1976, and the death of Steve Biko in 1977, led to a rise in the ANC's membership.
- The MK then stepped up its violent attacks:
  - The Sasolberg oil refinery (1980), Koeberg nuclear power station (1981) and Durban docks (1984) were all blown up by MK guerrillas.
  - The South African Defence Force (SADF) retaliated by bombing ANC bases and supporters in Angola and Mozambique.

The Pan African Congress (PAC)

- Many young black people felt that the ANC had been ineffective.
- Robert Sobukwe left the ANC and formed the PAC in 1959.
- The PAC called for **mass disobedience** rather than the **boycotts** and rallies organised by the ANC.
- The PAC organised a day of mass disobedience at Sharpeville on 21 March 1960.
    - Supporters were urged to refuse to carry passes and demand to be arrested.
    - When the crowd arrived at the police station the white police officers either panicked or deliberately fired at the crowd.
    - 69 protestors died and three times as many were injured. Most were shot in the back as they tried to escape.
- The Sharpeville Massacre boosted support for the PAC (and the ANC) and made their supporters even more determined to destroy apartheid.
- Meanwhile the United Nations (UN) condemned the South African government and international condemnation of apartheid began to gather momentum.

The Inkatha Freedom Party (IFP)

- Chief Buthelezi, Prime Minister of the KwaZulu Bantustan, created this Zulu-only organisation in 1975. It was committed to the creation of an independent Zulu nation.
- Many black Africans despised Chief Buthelezi because he appeared to be working alongside the National Party when he became leader of the KwaZulu Bantustan. PAC supporters tried to stone him in 1978.
- Chief Buthelezi's support came mainly from Zulu people who formed 40 per cent of the entire black population. It is not clear how much support Chief Buthelezi actually had among Zulus since he was never elected as their leader.
- The IFP was in direct opposition to the ANC who wanted a united South Africa. Throughout the 1980s and 1990s both groups engaged in bloody feuds that threatened the stability of the anti-apartheid movement.
- Both BOSS and the South African army (SADF – the South African Defense Force) exploited these divisions and is said to have arranged massacres on both sides in an attempt to spark a civil war between these two groups of black South Africans.

The United Democratic Front (UDF)

- In 1983 the UDF was formed in response to PW Botha's failure to get rid of apartheid in South Africa.
- 565 separate groups, including all races, colours, genders and religions, united in their determination to end apartheid once and for all.
- The UDF organised poster and leaflet campaigns and boycotts of elections that the National Party had hoped would satisfy non-white South Africans.

- Up until the 1980s the National Party had successfully divided opposition groups. However, the united UDF posed an enormous threat to the National Party's grip on South Africa.

What do I Know?

1 How did the ANC originally believe they could destroy apartheid?
2 Why was the Umkhonto we Sizwe (MK) formed?
3 What is mass disobedience?
4 When did the Sharpeville massacre take place?
5 Which party wanted an independent Zulu nation?
6 Why was the United Democratic Front seen as such a threat to the system of apartheid?

My score ....

Key Topic

How was the system of apartheid enforced?

- The National Party used an effective combination of laws and force to maintain apartheid and destroy opposition for over 40 years.

Laws 	Force
○ **1950 Suppression of Communism Act:** In reality this allowed the National Party to arrest and detain any individuals or groups deemed to be a threat to national security.	○ **The Sharpeville Massacre** and the deaths of over 1000 protesters in Soweto in 1976 demonstrate the violence the police forces, BOSS and SADF were prepared to use in attempts to maintain apartheid.
○ **1953 Bantu Education Act:** A poor education meant reduced opportunities for black people to challenge white-dominated business and other middle-class positions of power. The curriculum hoped to **indoctrinate** black people into accepting apartheid.	○ **Bureau of State Security** (BOSS): This was the South African secret police force that spied on opponents, infiltrated opposition groups and possibly carried out assassinations of key individuals.
○ **1960** The ANC and PAC were banned.	○ **South African Defence Force** (SADF): This was the South African army; it became more widely used during the 1980s when disturbances across South Africa meant that the police force and BOSS were unable to cope with the growing tide of opposition.
○ **1963** The government authorised the imprisonment of opponents for a period of 90 days without trial or legal representation. This was extended to 180 days in 1965.	○ The South African government and BOSS continually imprisoned, exiled and assassinated opponents of the apartheid system.
○ **Banning Orders:** Such orders were placed on opponents by South African courts. Those under a banning order might be placed under house arrest, be closely observed by police officers, have restrictions placed on their movement and be banned from making speeches or writing anti-Apartheid literature.	○ In the end the use of force by the South African government encouraged hatred and therefore even greater opposition.

How did the rest of the world react to apartheid?

- Despite the condemnation of South Africa by the UN in 1952, and its expulsion from the UN in 1974, most wealthy nations like Britain, Japan, France, Germany and the USA continued to trade with South Africa.
- South Africa's enormous gold, diamond and mineral reserves meant major industrial nations claimed they could not afford to boycott trade with South Africa.
- Foreign businesses and governments saw South Africa as an ideal investment because of its enormous mineral wealth and cheap human resources.
- The National Party's strong anti-communist stand brought support from both the USA and Britain during the Cold War.
- In the 1980s, Margaret Thatcher (British Prime Minister) and Ronald Reagan (US President) claimed that trade sanctions against South Africa were pointless since they would only hurt black South Africans.
- From the early 1970s onwards a worldwide boycott of South African sports teams meant the country was isolated from all tournaments and games until 1996.

What do I Know?

1 Which measures did the South African government use to restrict opposition to apartheid?
2 What was the aim of the Bantu Education Act?
3 How was opposition forcibly controlled in South Africa?
4 In what ways was South Africa punished for enforcing apartheid by foreign countries?
5 Why were foreign countries reluctant to boycott trade with South Africa?

My score ....

Key Topic

How and why was apartheid under threat by the late 1980s?

- When PW Botha became Prime Minister in September 1978 he claimed that South Africa had to 'adapt or die'.
- He saw South Africa, apartheid and the National Party facing a crisis for a number of reasons:
  - Modern farming methods that utilised new technology left millions of black farm labourers unemployed.
  - The Bantu Education Act created a generation of poorly educated blacks who were unable to operate increasingly complex factory machinery.
  - White factory owners complained that production was continually hampered by restrictions on recruiting black workers.
  - Black poverty meant that manufacturers were unable to sell their goods to the entire South African population.

- o Foreign companies like Barclays Bank began withdrawing their investments in protest against apartheid.
  - o A complete boycott of South Africa was looking more and more likely. This would have been a disaster because South Africa relied on exports.
- Under PW Botha, the National Party felt a growing sense of crisis and threat from forces inside South Africa and abroad.
- Botha particularly feared the threat of communism, following successful communist takeovers in nearby Angola and Mozambique. Botha also believed that the ANC and PAC were communists, backed by the Soviet Union.

'Total Strategy': Botha's attempt to save apartheid

- Botha aimed to 'Win Hearts And Minds' (WHAM) across black South Africa with reforms he hoped would satisfy opposition groups:
  - o Non-whites were permitted to join trade unions.
  - o All jobs were opened to non-whites on a permanent basis.
  - o Spending on black education tripled.
  - o Blacks were given greater freedom to move around South Africa and purchase homes and property in black townships.
  - o A new constitution was introduced in 1984 that gave limited voting rights to coloureds and Indians.
  - o Pass Laws were abolished.
  - o **'Petty Apartheid'** was abolished. This encouraged desegregation across South Africa and legalised mixed marriages.
- Botha believed these reforms would bring an end to the growing criticism against the National Party. However, his 'Total Strategy' did not go far enough to please many black or white South Africans:
  - o Political prisoners like Nelson Mandela remained in jail.
  - o Banning orders and internment remained.
  - o BOSS and SADF continued with their activities.
  - o Non-whites were not given voting rights equal to those of white South Africans.
  - o Black and white housing remained divided.
  - o White students still received a better education than non-white children.
- Botha's Total Strategy also aimed to destroy all threats to National Party rule:
  - o Police powers were increased to stop, search, arrest and detain anyone without trial.
  - o There was increased censorship, curfews and detention of suspected opponents.
  - o Military spending was quadrupled.
  - o Compulsory military service amongst whites was extended.

- BOSS assassinated leading ANC leaders in exile.
- The State Security Council (SSC) was created. This was a body of military figures who plotted to eliminate all opponents of apartheid.
- Military training camps for youths were set up.
- The South African arms industry was created, known as 'ARMSCOR'.

What was the impact of Botha's 'Total Strategy'?

- Botha's Total Strategy actually had the opposite effect to what was desired. Opposition to both apartheid and the National Party grew rapidly.
  - Thousands of blacks flocked to South Africa's urban centres and built temporary squatter camps on the edges of towns and cities. These became breeding grounds for ANC and PAC support.
  - Elections to South Africa's new government were successfully boycotted.
  - Ultra-right-wing supporters of the National Party were horrified by Botha's reforms. Many left to join the Conservative Party which promised to maintain traditional apartheid laws.
  - Non-whites were actually encouraged by Botha's reforms. They saw the changes as evidence of the impending collapse of apartheid.
- The Total Strategy encouraged opponents of apartheid and began to create major divisions within the National Party itself.
- By 1985, worldwide economic sanctions were beginning to have a serious effect on the South African economy.
- Major American and European banks began to refuse loans to South Africa and demanded immediate repayment of previous loans. This was because their own customers were threatening to only invest in banks that boycotted South Africa.
- The sudden repayment of loans in 1985-6 had a devastating impact on the South African economy and plunged the country into a recession.
- PW Botha began receiving complaints from the white business communities which were badly affected by the foreign boycotts.

What do I Know?

1 What were the two strands of Botha's Total Strategy?
2 Describe the key features of PW Botha's 'WHAM' reforms.
3 How did PW Botha attempt to rid the National Party of its enemies?
4 Why did some National Party supporters leave the Party?

My score ....

Key Topic

What was life like in South Africa during the state of emergency?

- In September 1984 a small protest in a township outside Johannesburg escalated into a major uprising that spread across South Africa.
- By 1985 townships across South Africa witnessed continued disturbances against apartheid. This resulted in Botha declaring a state of emergency, which lasted five years.
- The state of emergency increased police and army powers to stop, arrest and imprison anyone suspected of being a threat to national security.
- Confrontations and street battles between protesters and the police or SADF increased. By 1989 nearly 4000 people had been killed and up to 20,000 had been injured.
- Chaos and disorder became uncontrollable across South Africa. Both the National Party and their opponents sensed the country was on the verge of a civil war.
- Following a stroke Botha resigned and was replaced by the moderate FW de Klerk in August 1989.

How was apartheid brought to an end?

- De Klerk believed that South Africa had to reform its laws and policies because:
  - South Africa was on the verge of civil war.
  - The National Party was losing support from the moderate and extreme wings of its own party.
  - The South African economy had been in decline for nearly five years.
  - The end of the Cold War meant foreign governments no longer needed South Africa's support against communism.
- De Klerk understood that greater power sharing had to take place if South Africa were to avoid civil war.
- In February 1990 De Klerk shocked the world with three announcements:
  1. The legalisation of the ANC and PAC.
  2. The immediate release of Nelson Mandela and other political prisoners.
  3. A promise of equal rights for all South Africans.
- Again the more extreme supporters of the National Party abandoned De Klerk and joined extremist groups like the Conservative Party or Eugene Terre Blanche's **neo-Nazi** style party, Afrikaner Weerstandsbeweging (AWB).
- Nevertheless, in a referendum in 1992 over two-thirds of all white South Africans declared their support for De Klerk's reforms.
- In April 1994 the first ever democratic elections in South African history took place. The ANC won and Nelson Mandela became South Africa's new President.

- The following month the new South African government met. This included representatives from the ANC, the National Party and the Inkatha Freedom Party.

▲ **Nelson Mandela**   ▲ **FW De Klerk**   ▲ **Chief Buthelezi**   ▲ **Terre Blanche**   ▲ **Desmond Tutu**

How did Nelson Mandela go from prisoner to President?

- On 1 February 1990 Mandela walked free after 26 years in prison.
- On 10 May 1994 Mandela became President of South Africa. For many this was just a natural progression for the internationally known ANC member. However, the time between his release and the election was bitter and filled with disagreement.
- The ANC and National Party met in May 1990 and immediately disagreed on the kind of elections that should take place.
  - The ANC wanted a simple 'one-person one-vote' system. This would have ensured an end to the National Party's power.
  - The National Party opposed any election that might threaten white influence in South Africa's future.
- The National Party and the ANC still did not trust one another:
  - Some members of the National Party viewed the ANC as communist terrorists and saboteurs.
  - Many in the ANC despised the National Party for authorising assassinations, arrest, exiles and years of brutality and oppression.
  - In addition the ANC suspected that the National Party were delaying agreement on future elections in the hope that civil war would erupt between the ANC and the Inkatha Freedom Party.
- Both the National Party and the ANC were bitterly opposed by sections of the black and white communities:
  - The National Party became increasingly concerned by the armed threat of Eugene Terre Blanche's AWB.
  - The ANC were opposed by the IFP who claimed that the ANC did not represent the majority of black South Africans.
  - Chief Buthelezi, leader of the IFP, demanded an independent homeland for the Zulu people and threatened to boycott any future elections to a new South African government.

- Between 1990 and 1994 terrible violence broke out again across South Africa, particularly between ANC and IFP supporters. Hundreds were butchered with 'pangas' (a long machete type knife) and the violence threatened to spill over into a civil war.
- White extremists assassinated Chris Hani, the popular leader of the MK.
- In March 1993 talks reopened and a final solution was reached.
  - The National Party was appeased with guarantees that any party that got over 20 per cent of the vote would be guaranteed a deputy president.
  - Similarly, any party with over 5 per cent of the vote would be given the right to appoint a member of the government's cabinet.
- Despite an AWB attempt to organise a coup in Bophutswana prior to the election, all the major political parties took part.
- The April 1994 election results were as follows:
  - ANC   62.5 per cent (Mandela became President)
  - National Party 20.5 per cent (De Klerk became Deputy President)
  - IFP   10.5 per cent (Buthelezi became a cabinet minister in Mandela's government)

What do I Know?

1 When did De Klerk become President?
2 Why did De Klerk start to reform laws in South Africa?
3 Which three changes did De Klerk announce in February 1990?
4 Did the ANC and National Party represent the interests of all South Africans?
5 When did the first democratic elections take place in South Africa?
6 What percentage of the vote went to the ANC?

My score ....

Key Words and Names

Apartheid
Means 'separateness' and describes the laws introduced by the National Party since 1948 to segregate people of different races.

Boers
Means 'farmers'. This name was given to the descendants of the original Dutch settlers to South Africa.

BOSS
The Bureau Of State Security; the South African secret police force.

Boycott
An organised agreement to end all economic, cultural or sporting relations with another country.

Indoctrinate
An attempt to 'brainwash' or influence the values and opinions of another person.

Nelson Mandela
ANC anti–apartheid activist, jailed in 1962. He later became South African President.

Mass disobedience
Deliberately breaking laws considered to be unfair or immoral, for example, carrying pass books or sitting on 'whites only' park benches. Such campaigns are intended to lead to mass arrests and collapse of the state's justice system.

Neo-Nazi
Extreme right-wing groups that adopt Nazi-style flags, uniforms, slogans and values.

Pass Laws
Measures introduced by the National Party to restrict the movement of non–white people in South Africa.

Petty apartheid
Aspects of apartheid that were considered either unworkable or a nuisance to both black and white communities. For example, preventing the employment of blacks in industry.

Puppet leaders
This describes any leader or government that appears to hold power but is in fact controlled by another country or authority.

Walter Sisulu
ANC leader jailed along with Nelson Mandela and released in October 1989.

State of emergency
This gives governments enormous powers to bring a situation under control and restore government control. They are often declared following natural disasters or during wars and uprisings.

Soweto Schools Uprising
Began as a black student protest in 1976 against the poor education system. The police reacted by shooting between 600 and 1000 demonstrators.

Desmond Tutu
Anglican priest and anti-apartheid campaigner. He won the Nobel Peace Prize in 1984 and then became Archbishop of Cape Town in 1986.

Exam Type Questions

Study the sources and questions carefully. Attempt the questions yourself, then compare your answers with the answers given and check the examiner's comments.

Source A

> Can we abandon a country that has stood behind us in every war we've ever fought, a country that is strategically essential to the free world? It has production of minerals we must have. I feel that if we are going to sit down at a table and negotiate with Russians, then surely we can keep the door open and negotiate with a friendly nation like South Africa.

▲ **An extract of a speech by US President Ronald Reagan in 1981.**

Source B

▲ **Members of the Black Sash protesting in Johannesburg against apartheid.**

> **1** What can you learn from Source A about why the USA was reluctant to impose economic sanctions on South Africa?

Answer 1

Reagan is trying to argue that South Africa was too important for the USA to make an enemy of. Reagan points out that the USA relied on South Africa for the import of essential chemicals and minerals. Also he refers to the 'strategically essential' position of South Africa. This is a reference to South Africa's determined attempt to crush communist governments in neighbouring countries like Angola and Mozambique. In 1981 the USA was very worried about the growth of communism in South America and southern Africa.

Examiner's Comments on: Answer 1

4 out of 4

The candidate's background knowledge places the source in the context of world affairs at the time. Therefore he/she is able to infer Reagan's basic arguments against economic sanctions.

> **2** How useful is Source B as evidence about opposition to apartheid in South Africa?

Answer 2

The photograph only gives us an impression of a small group of opponents from a relatively small section of the anti-apartheid movement. These Black Sash members (an organisation of white middle-class opponents of apartheid) appear to be calling for an end to the state of emergency ('UPHOLD THE RULE OF LAW') and an end to the restrictions on opponents' movements ('STOP BANNING'). The photograph could be used to show how deep-rooted opposition was across all South African communities or to mock the efforts of five rather isolated looking protesters. Either way the photograph does not show us the scale of opposition or represent the aims of the entire anti-apartheid movement.

Examiner's Comments on: Answer 2

3 out of 3

The candidate successfully judges the limitations of this source by referring to its nature and uncertain purpose. The candidate wisely suggests alternative purposes for the source rather than ignoring the issue entirely. A source can have more than one purpose, depending on how and when it is used.

> **3** Using Sources A and B and your own knowledge explain why De Klerk agreed to end apartheid.

Answer 3

By the late 1980s Reagan's arguments (Source A) to avoid sanctions against South Africa no longer applied. Public opinion across the world had shifted so much against apartheid that no leader would dare defend the South African government. Also the threat of communism began to pass with its collapse in the USSR and eastern Europe in 1990-1. Therefore South Africa was under tremendous pressure to introduce comprehensive reforms. Source B indicates the sheer scale of anti-apartheid protests within South Africa. Opponents now came from white middle-class communities - the traditional supporters of the National Party and defenders of the apartheid regime. De Klerk simply responded to the growing criticism of apartheid inside and outside of South Africa.

Examiner's Comments on: Answer 3

4 out of 5

The candidate uses the sources effectively but makes the common mistake of not introducing sufficient knowledge. The candidate could have referred to foreign factors such as the withdrawal of foreign companies like Barclays Bank or the economic recession that had lasted since 1985. In addition, South Africa was on the verge of civil war as black communities rose up against the South African army and police force.

Practice Questions

1 What can you learn from Source B about the treatment of blacks in South Africa?
   HINT: What are the placards referring to?
2 How useful is Source A as evidence about why foreign countries were slow to place economic sanctions on South Africa?
   HINT: Look at the origin of this source.
3 Using Sources A and B and your own knowledge explain why apartheid remained intact for over 40 years.
   HINT: Were Reagan's reasons still valid by the 1990s?

8. Nationalism and independence in India, c.1900–49

Topic Summary

In 1900 opposition to British rule in India was virtually non-existent. However over a period of almost 50 years a series of massacres, broken promises and slow reforms gradually destroyed Indian respect for British rule and encouraged the growth of powerful opposition groups. At first, opposition was united. However by the 1930s Hindus and Muslims were as suspicious of one another as they were of the British. This denied India a peaceful transition towards independence. The eventual partition of India was to become the most harrowing period in India's long history.

What do I Need to Know?

You will need to know how India gradually moved towards independence and partition between c.1900 and 1947. This will include an understanding of why opposition to British rule grew, why Hindus and Muslims became divided and the series of reforms that gradually saw a decline in British power.

Key Topics

1 India in 1900

The background

- British power in India had grown steadily since the early seventeenth century.
- In 1600 Elizabeth I granted the foundation of the East India Company. This controlled trade with India until the Great Mutiny of 1857–8.
- The Great Mutiny shocked the British government which then reorganised control of their Indian colony.
- In 1858 India was placed under direct British control and in 1877 Queen Victoria was proclaimed the Empress of India.
- British control over India then became known as the **Raj**, until independence in 1947.

How was India ruled under the British Raj?

- India was ruled by the **Viceroy**.
- His rule was supported with over 70,000 civil servants.
- 2 million soldiers in the Indian army maintained the rule of British law and suppressed any would-be rebels.

Raj

A Hindi word meaning 'rule'.

Viceroy

Means 'deputy king'.

- The entire costs of the British Raj and the upkeep of the Indian army were paid through taxes collected from the Indian people.
- 40 per cent of India was made up of princely states. Princes were given Home Rule in return for their support of British rule.
- Representatives of the British government ruled the other 60 per cent of India:
  - The Viceroy had the power to rule by decree; whatever he said was law.
  - The Viceroy was supported by an advisory group of five men known as the Executive Council.
  - An Imperial Legislative Council was created to offer advice and opinions on behalf of India's enormous population.
  - India was then split into dozens of smaller provinces, ruled by a governor or lieutenant governor.
  - Each province was divided into districts that were administered by members of the Indian Civil Service (ICS).
- The Viceroy was required to report back to the Secretary of State for India, who was a member of the British prime minister's cabinet in London.
- In conclusion, all power lay in British hands. Indians were not given the right to vote or the power to propose or reject new laws.

Initial opposition to the Raj

- Throughout the remainder of the nineteenth century there was surprisingly little opposition to British rule.
  - The princely states were content to be left alone.
  - Indian farmers were more interested in ensuring successful harvests.
  - The emerging Indian middle classes wanted to work with the British Raj rather than overthrow it.
  - The Indian army frightened off would-be rebels.
- The **Indian National Congress (INC)** was founded in 1885 but made very little impact until the twentieth century.

Indian National Congress
This is often referred to as 'Congress'.

Why was India so important to the British?

- India was nicknamed the 'brightest jewel in the imperial crown'.
- This reputation was based on the enormous wealth India brought to Britain:
  - Indians' taxes paid for the entire British Raj.
  - India provided an inexhaustible supply of soldiers.
  - India was a very cheap source of raw materials whilst providing an enormous market for British manufactured goods: one-fifth of all British exports went to India.
  - 37,000 km (23,000 miles) of railways and 110,000 km (70,000 miles) of canals were constructed to encourage the import and export of goods across India.

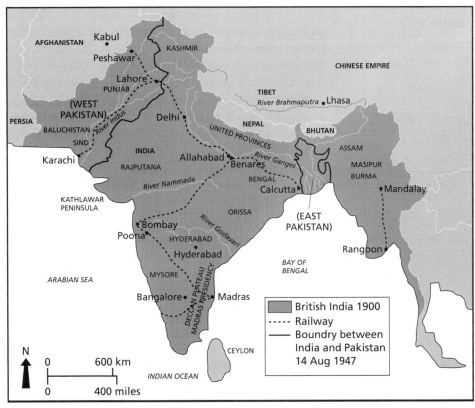

▲ **Map of India in 1900, showing princely states and main cities.**

Key Topic

2 The partition of Bengal and the growth of Indian opposition

Viceroy Curzon

- In 1900 there was little organised or popular anti-British feeling in India. This was all about to change.
- In 1905, Lord Curzon divided the province of Bengal into separate Hindu and Muslim areas, without consultation. Bengal was now divided into 'East Bengal' and 'West Bengal'.
- He did this because Bengal had a population of nearly 80 million and was therefore too big to govern effectively as a single province.
- The Hindus reacted angrily because they now became a minority group in East Bengal and feared Muslim intimidation.

The impact of the partition of Bengal

- Congress became the national voice of Indian resentment towards the British.
- Congress tried to force Lord Curzon to reverse his decision by calling for a **swadeshi** campaign. This encouraged supporters to:
  - Boycott British imports.
  - Burn any imported goods like clothes and luxury goods.

Swadeshi

A campaign aimed at boycotting the sale or purchase of non-Indian goods.

Cottage industry

Small scale, family-run business.

Invoke

To introduce temporary powers only available in an emergency.

- India's **cottage industries** were boosted by the swadeshi campaign because they suddenly found markets for traditional Indian shoes, glassware, sugar and soap.
- Congress condemned acts of violence (like rioting and the destruction of property) as a means of forcing change.
- As the campaign continued, supporters of Congress began rioting in East Bengal and the Punjab. Some carried out bomb attacks and made four unsuccessful assassination attempts on Lord Curzon.
- Whilst the vast majority of India continued to live and work as before, localised trouble spots forced Lord Curzon to **invoke** the Police Act:
  - Streets were cleared of protesters by the Indian army.
  - Activists were arrested.
  - Public meetings were banned.
  - Strict censorship measures were introduced.
- In 1906, leaders of Congress demanded Home Rule for the first time.

The foundation of the Muslim League (1906)

- The violence of Congress extremist supporters was directed against both the British and Muslims.
- Consequently the All-India Muslim League was formed in 1906. Like Congress, they made moderate demands and rejected violence.
- Initially the Muslim League had three aims:
  - To promote loyalty among Muslims towards the British Empire.
  - To protect the political and civil rights of Indian Muslims.
  - To tackle hostility among Muslims towards other Indian religions.

The Morley-Minto Reforms, 1909

- Finally the British government introduced the Indian Councils Act (better known as the Morley-Minto Reforms) in an attempt to curb growing opposition within India.
- It was the first step in the eventual withdrawal of all British power:
  - Indians were admitted onto the Imperial Executive Council and the Imperial Legislative Council.
  - The Council remained as an advisory body without lawmaking powers. The Congress called it a 'powerless talking shop'.
  - Provincial assemblies (or '**legislatures**') were to be elected by the Indian people. They sat alongside appointed British civil servants and in some cases were in a majority – therefore allowing some changes to be introduced.
  - Guaranteed seats for minority groups, such as Muslims and Sikhs, were granted in both the Imperial Legislative Council and the provincial assemblies.

Legislatures

Government assemblies with powers to reform or introduce new laws.

- The reforms were welcomed as a step in the right direction but had not gone far enough:
  - Only 2 per cent of Indians had the vote (the wealthiest and best educated).
  - Real lawmaking powers still rested in the hands of the British.
- Peace was finally restored in 1911 when Curzon decided to reverse the partition of Bengal. On the surface things looked back to normal.

Summary Box 1

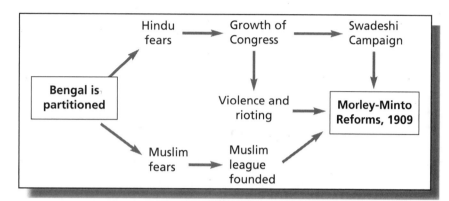

What do I Know?

1 Who governed most of India at the end of the nineteenth century?
2 Give three reasons why the British were so keen to maintain their control over India.
3 Why did Hindus react angrily to the partition of Bengal?
4 What three aims did the Muslim League have?
5 Who was admitted to the Imperial Legislative Council as a result of the Morley-Minto reforms?

My score ....

Key Topic

3 The impact of the First World War

How did India contribute to the British war effort?

- The Viceroy declared war on the Central Powers (Germany, Austria-Hungary and later Turkey) on behalf of 300 million Indians under his control.
- During the war 1,440,437 Indians volunteered, 62,000 of whom died.
- At first the Indian economy benefited from the war because there was a vast increase in exports of blankets, tents, shoes and munitions to Britain. The cloth industry in particular benefited and encouraged the growth of cottage industries.
- Taxes were raised without much opposition. In addition, £3 million was donated to the war effort.
- The war also created jobs in the new iron and steel plants that had sprung up across India, for example the huge 'Tata' plant at Jamshedpur.

Home Rule

When a former colony is granted powers to run its own affairs.

Dominion status

When a former colony's government operates without British interference but retains the British monarch as the head of state.

Did the war change Indian politics?

- At the beginning of the war both Congress and the Muslim League declared their support for the war, hoping to be rewarded for their loyalty with **Home Rule** at the end of the war.
- However some Indians were opposed to the war:
  - Many Indian Muslims opposed fighting against the Turkish Muslims.
  - Heavy taxes hit the poorest farmers.
  - Inflation spread throughout India and wiped out savings and harvest profits.

The Lucknow Pact (April 1916)

- In April 1916, the Lucknow Pact was agreed by the leaders of Congress (Motilal Nehru) and the Muslim League (Mohammed Ali Jinnah). The pact was intended to represent a peaceful and progressive vision of India after the war.
- Both Congress and the Muslim League aimed to form a new India with **dominion status** within the British Empire.
- Both agreed to respect the other's religion.
- The Muslim League's demand for a fixed number of Muslim seats in a future Indian government was accepted.

The Montagu Declaration

- On 20 August 1917 the new Secretary of State for India, Lord Montagu, issued the Montagu Declaration, outlining his vision for post-war India:
  - 'Increasing associations of Indians in every branch of government.'
  - 'The development of self governing institutions.'
  - 'The progressive realisation of representative government in India.'
- India's loyalty in the war appeared to be on the verge of being rewarded.

Key Topic

4 1919 – the turning point?

The Montagu-Chelmsford Reforms (1919) and the birth of the Dyarchy

- Montagu made his Declaration without the approval of the British government.
- He was forced to compromise and with Viceroy Chelmsford proposed the Montagu-Chelmsford Reforms, which became known in 1919 as the Government of India Act.
- The reforms were an attempt to begin giving Indians a limited voice on how India was governed.

- The reforms changed India's government:
  - The Imperial Executive Council remained without any law making powers but now included three Indians.
  - The Legislative Assembly and the Upper House replaced the Imperial Legislative Council. Neither had law making powers and were simply there to offer advice to the viceroy.

  The majority of the Legislative Assembly's 146 members were to be freely elected; however, it too was a purely advisory body.
  - The Upper House represented the views of India's wealthiest communities – usually princes or wealthy landowners.
  - The provincial assemblies were given much greater power and generally run by elected Indians. These assemblies were given freedom to control departments such as education, healthcare and transport.
  - The Viceroy retained control of national issues such as law and order, foreign policy and taxation.
- This system of government was called a 'Dyarchy' and seen as a step towards the eventual independence of India. On one hand it gave new powers to the Indian people, but it also retained control of others.
- Voting rights were extended from 2 per cent to 3.3 per cent of the total adult population.
- Compared with the Montagu Declaration, the Montagu-Chelmsford Reforms were seen as a disappointing anticlimax. Nevertheless, Congress and the Muslim League welcomed the reforms as another step in the right direction.

The Rowlatt Acts (March 1919)

- In 1915 the Defence of India Act was reintroduced as a wartime emergency. The law gave the government powers of arrest and imprisonment of anyone suspected of being a threat to national security. Despite repeated protests, the Act was generally accepted during wartime amongst Indians.
- In March 1919, Sir Charles Rowlatt, chair of a committee investigating the continued use of the Defence of India Act in peacetime, proposed the Rowlatt **Bill**.
- His bill extended the Defence of India Act into peacetime.
- Despite fierce opposition the bill became law on 18 March 1919.
- Jinnah and other nationalist leaders stormed out of the Legislative Assembly in protest.
- The Rowlatt Acts were widely condemned as:
  - A deliberate attempt to prevent free expression and the rights of Indians to determine the future of their country.
  - An insult to Indian loyalty during the First World War.
- The Rowlatt Acts were never used, but again damaged Indian faith in British rule.

Act

An actual change in the law.

Bill

A proposed change in the law.

(handwritten margin notes: No law making power; Imperial Executive council; Legislative assembly; Upper house; Provincial assemblies; advisory body; Power)

The Amritsar Massacre (April 1919)

Part one: Growing tension

- On 10 April 1919, the deputy commissioner in Amritsar, faced a 40,000 strong riot in opposition to his decision to expel two Congress members from the city.
- 25 Indians and five British soldiers were killed in the riot.
- On 11 April Brigadier-General Dyer was called in to take charge of the armed forces.
- By 13 April the city was crowded with traders from the local countryside.
- On the same day Dyer:
  - Prohibited anyone leaving the city without a permit.
  - Introduced a curfew to last from 8.00pm until daybreak.
  - Outlawed public gatherings of any sort, political or religious.

Part two: The day of the massacre

- On 13 April, at 5.15pm, Dyer and 130 armed soldiers arrived at a protest meeting of between 5000 and 15,000 Indians, in an enclosed courtyard called Jallianwalla Bagh.
- Without warning the troops opened fire. Within ten minutes 379 men, women and children had died and over 1200 lay wounded.
- The crowd had dispersed in terror and Dyer retreated with his men to their barracks.
- Medical services were virtually non-existent and were prevented from helping the injured.
- When the curfew began at 8.00pm, the dead and wounded lay until the morning when families were finally able to search the site for relatives.

Part three: The aftermath of the massacre

- In the weeks that followed, Indian public opinion was further outraged:
  - Across the Punjab region British army officials restricted travel, ordered public floggings and imprisoned innocent people.
  - Strict censorship attempted to cover up the massacre.
  - British soldiers allegedly slaughtered sacred cows, pigeons and other birds as deliberate acts of sacrilege against the Hindu faith.
  - Air raids were carried out on Indian villages such as Dhulla and Gharjakh.

Part four: The impact on public opinion

- The Indian people were not only enraged by the massacre but also by the British reaction to it:
  - Parts of the British press called Dyer the 'Saviour of the Empire'.
  - The British House of Lords praised and approved of Dyer's actions.
  - The Hunter Report (the British investigation into the Amritsar massacre) described Dyer's actions as 'frightful' and that he '… offended against every canon of civilised government'. Nevertheless Dyer did not go to prison.
  - British newspapers like the *Morning Post* organised public contributions for 'the man who saved India'.
- The events at Amritsar slowly emerged from the Punjab region and had a dramatic effect on public opinion towards British rule.
- Indians lost faith in British justice and joined campaigns for independence from British rule.
- Gandhi summed up the feelings of most Indians when he said,

… nothing less than the removal of the British and complete self-government can satisfy injured India.

What do I Know?

1 How many Indians volunteered to fight during the First World War?
2 List the reforms brought about by the Montagu-Chelmsford reforms.
3 What was the 'Dyarchy'?
4 Which acts extended the Defence of India Act into peacetime?
5 When did the Amritsar Massacre take place?

My score ………

Key Topic

5 Opposition to British Rule, 1920–7

The emergence of Gandhi (1920)

- In 1920 Mohandas Gandhi became the most important leader in Congress.
- Between 1893 and 1915 Gandhi had worked with South African Indians, who were also campaigning for civil rights.
- Whilst in South Africa he had developed the satyagraha movement, meaning 'soul force', which included his Seven Points:
  1 Indians to surrender titles and honours bestowed by the Raj.
  2 The boycott of official state functions.
  3 The removal of children from state schools.
  4 Indian lawyers to boycott the courts.
  5 Refusal to join the Indian army.
  6 Boycott any elections.
  7 Boycott the purchase of foreign goods.

- In 1920, Gandhi introduced reforms within Congress that again increased its support:
  - He called for 'swaraj' or Home Rule.
  - He permitted involvement of the lowest Hindu castes in the movement (approximately 45 million in 1920).
  - He organised a civil disobedience campaign.
  - He encouraged a return to traditional Indian costume, foods, traditions and goods as a rejection of all things British. This was called the swadeshi campaign.

Gandhi's Non-Cooperation or Satyagraha Campaign (1920–2)

- Gandhi encouraged huge bonfires of British-made goods.
- Thousands of charkhas or spinning wheels were handed out to encourage the hand weaving of homespun cotton and wool.
- Throughout India, boycotts of the elections and non-purchase of imports proved very effective.
- However, by the end of 1921 Gandhi's prediction of swaraj looked doomed. The British policy to ignore protests, known as non-interference, proved very effective.
- By mid 1921 the Indian people began fighting among themselves:
  - The Moplahs, a group of Muslims from southern India, declared a **jihad** against local Hindus. 4000 Moplahs and 100 troops died before the Indian army put down their revolt.
  - Between 1920 and 1926 over 120 major riots broke out between Hindus and Muslims.
- In an attempt to keep the campaign alive, Gandhi called for a second phase of the campaign, known as active civil disobedience.
  - This began as a boycott of the Prince of Wales' visit to Bombay in November 1921.
  - Along the coastline from the arrival of the Prince, Gandhi encouraged the burning of imported British goods.
  - Despite his calls for non-violence, the crowds fought fellow Indians who had ignored the boycott of the royal visit and were now returning home.
  - In the five days of rioting that followed, 59 people were killed. Gandhi postponed his civil disobedience campaign and declared a fast, to cleanse the sins of the Indian people.

The Chauri Chaura incident and the collapse of the Satyagraha Campaign

- The Raj responded by calling off its non-interference policy and by 1922 had arrested 30,000 Congress supporters.
- Gandhi was not arrested and he called for another local civil disobedience campaign in Bardoli.

jihad

Holy Islamic war.

Ashram

An Indian retreat aimed at encouraging learning and spiritual growth.

Untouchables

Re-named the 'children of God' by Gandhi. These Hindus were outside the caste system and deemed the lowest class of Hindu. Sharing food and water with an untouchable, or even walking through their shadow, was believed by many to be enough to permanently poison a Hindu soul.

- However, in the village of Chauri Chaura, just outside Bardoli, 2000 supporters of Congress besieged the local police station and burned to death 21 officers inside.
- Gandhi immediately called an end to the entire campaign.
- Gandhi was arrested on 10 March 1922 and charged with 'bringing into hatred or contempt the government established by law in the British Empire'. Gandhi pleaded guilty and was sentenced to six years in prison.
- In the years between 1924 and 1928 Gandhi founded an **'ashram'** in Gujerat that encouraged the regeneration of traditional Indian crafts and aimed to improve the lives of the **'Untouchables'**.

How did the imprisonment of Gandhi affect Congress?

- Whilst Gandhi remained in his ashram, Congress began to split and two new leaders emerged: Motilal and Jawaharlal Nehru, who were father and son.
- Motilal Nehru created a splinter group within Congress called the Swaraj Party (Home Rule Party). It believed in working closely with the British.
- Motila's son, Jawaharlal, founded the Non-Cooperation Movement. Jawaharlal had little faith in working alongside the British.
- In the November 1923 elections, the Swaraj Party were very successful and formed the Nationalist Bloc with Jinnah's Muslim League.
- After 1923, the British were thus faced with a united opposition to British rule.
- This allowed India to begin breaking Britain's control over the finances of their country:
  - Entrance exams to the Indian Civil Service were to be held in New Delhi as well as London. It was hoped this would equalise the number of British and Indian members.
  - India was given the power to set import tariffs and to restrict the import of British goods, which had stunted the growth of Indian industry.
  - The Indian army was only to be used in campaigns within the borders of India.
  - India's spending plans no longer needed British Cabinet approval.
- By 1927 British power had begun to decline but remained the central force in Indian politics.

Key Topic

6 The impact of the Simon Commission

The arrival of the commission

- In 1927 a commission led by Sir John Simon was sent to investigate the workings of the 1919 Montagu-Chelmsford Reforms and to recommend any necessary changes to the government of India.

- The commission started badly when the British government failed to name a single Indian delegate. This was seen as an insult and a snub.
- The commission recommended a federal India and that each province would have its own government, but that central government would not be changed. This meant that there were no real proposals to change the way India was governed.
- Congress responded with a boycott of the commission. When the commission arrived they were met with thousands of protesters holding banners that read 'Simon Go Back!'
- The majority of the Muslim League denounced the Simon Commission. Jinnah urged supporters to 'have nothing to do with the commission'.
- Mass demonstrations followed the commission wherever they went. This was accompanied by major strikes across India.

The Nehru Report (July 1928)

- In July 1928 Congress met to propose their own future government of India. It became known as the 'Nehru Report' and made a series of basic demands:
  - India was to become a federal state.
  - There would be a powerful central government with power over all federal states.
  - Universal franchise or votes for everyone.
  - Immediate dominion status.
- Congress and the Muslim League approved the Nehru Report, despite Jinnah's protests. Jinnah wanted total independence and greater power for Muslims.
- The end of 1928 was a major turning point:
  - More radical leaders in Congress, like Jawaharlal Nehru and Subhas Chandra Bose, had little faith in working with the British and called for complete independence.
  - Gandhi avoided a split within Congress by brokering a compromise that gave the British a one-year ultimatum to introduce full dominion status, otherwise independence or **purna swaraj** would become the aim of Congress.

Major divisions between Congress and the Muslim League

- Before the 1930s most members of the Muslim League were also members of Congress. It was not until the 1930s that Congress was seen as a Hindu-only party.
- In December 1928 Jinnah urged the annual Congress conference to call for decentralised power in any new Indian government. That way he hoped a Hindu-dominated national government would not interfere with local Muslim communities. However, Congress rejected Jinnah's ideas.
- This was the start of the split that eventually resulted in the breakaway state of Pakistan.

---

purna swaraj

The Indian term for 'complete independence'.

- Jinnah began to believe that the interests of India's Muslims would be better served by closer cooperation with the British rather than Congress.
- When the Simon Report was finally published in June 1930 it suggested:
  - The replacement of the Dyarchy with a federal style of government.
  - The viceroy to maintain power over foreign policy, the Indian Civil Service, police and armed forces.
- Congress condemned the Report. However, Jinnah and the Muslim League coolly welcomed it, mainly because it proposed a federal state that would give power to local Muslims.

Gandhi's Second Satyagraha Campaign, 1929–31

- At the December annual meeting of Congress in 1929, the one-year ultimatum for purna swaraj had expired.
- Rather than waiting for the Simon Report to be published in June 1930 (its content had been widely leaked anyway), Congress declared independence as its goal and announced the start of the civil disobedience campaign.
- Gandhi also declared the beginning of the second Satyagraha campaign. Gandhi hoped that through non-violent methods India would become completely ungovernable.
- The most memorable feature of the campaign was Gandhi's March to the Sea:
  - This twenty-four day march to the shores of Dandi culminated in Gandhi symbolically lifting a lump of sea salt from the beach.
  - This was a violation of the Salt Laws, which forbade the production of salt without a government licence.
  - By the end of the morning 320 people in the crowd had been beaten by the police and two had been killed.
  - Gandhi was arrested on 4 May 1930 but, despite this, 5 million Indians began making their own salt in defiance of British rule.
- Across India, British goods were boycotted, shops picketed, taxes left unpaid and local Indian officials went on strike.
- By the end of the year, 100,000 Indians had been arrested, strikes paralysed major industries, foreign imports dried up and at least 100 Indians had been shot dead by the police.
- Despite Gandhi's call for non-violence, a number of riots did break out, especially in Bengal and the Punjab where dozens of local magistrates and other British civil servants were murdered.
- However, Jinnah and the majority of Muslims opposed the civil disobedience and Satyagraha campaigns. Jinnah convinced Muslims that they would be better off working with, and gaining the respect of, the British.

What do I Know?

1 What does 'swaraj' mean?
2 List the key features of Gandhi's Satyagraha Campaign of 1920-2.
3 Name the two men who emerged as leaders of Congress in the late 1920s.
4 What did the Simon Commission propose?
5 What did the Nehru Report propose?
6 When did Gandhi's 'March to the Sea' take place?

My score ....

Key Topic

7 The Round Table Conferences and their impact

- In June 1930 the British government called for a 'Round Table' conference in London. This was an attempt to try to reach an agreement on how India should be governed.

The Round Table conferences

- India faced a series of problems that clearly needed to be tackled:
  - The Dyarchy, set up in 1919, was not working.
  - The Simon Report had proved a total failure.
  - 40 per cent of India was still ruled by princes.
  - There was increasing tension between Muslim and Hindu communities.
  - The once moderate Congress had become more extreme.

The First Round Table Conference – November 1930

- Congress refused to send a representative until immediate dominion status was granted.
- Representatives from the Muslim League and 16 Indian princes did attend.
- Agreement was reached to form a federal state, along the lines of the USA.
- The conference ended because no firm agreement could be reached whilst Congress was kept away from the talks (many of its members were in prison).

The Second Round Table Conference – September 1931

- Gandhi was released from prison and agreed to take part in talks with the Indian government.
- The conference collapsed and Gandhi reintroduced the civil disobedience campaign.

The Communal Award – August 1932

- In August 1932 the British declared a Communal Award that gave separate and guaranteed seats, in any Indian assembly, to represent the interests of Muslims, Sikhs, Christians and, most controversially, the 50 million Untouchables.
- Gandhi feared the British were trying to divide the people of India in their struggle against British rule. Gandhi wanted Congress to be a single voice for all Indian people in their struggle for independence.
- When the leader of the Untouchables, BR Ambedkar, welcomed the Communal Award, Gandhi threatened to fast to death unless he withdrew his support.
- Following intense pressure, Ambedkar rejected the Communal Award.

The Third Round Table Conference – November 1932

- Neither Congress nor any of the major princely states sent a representative to this conference. Jinnah was not even invited, nor the British Labour Party.
- The conference again focused on who would have the vote and how much each federal state would have.
- Again the conference broke up without agreement.
- By 1935 the British government introduced the Government of India Act that finally gave Indians real power over their country.

The Government of India Act (1935)

- The Act was a combination of both the Simon Report and the Round Table conferences.
- The Act set up a new Indian government as follows:
  - A national parliament would be created in Delhi with two chambers, the 'Council of State' and the 'Assembly'.
  - Both chambers would have a combination of appointed members who would be outnumbered by elected members. All elected members would be Indian.
  - The rest of India would be split into 11 separate provinces that would control everything except defence and foreign policy; these matters were to remain under the control of the viceroy. The viceroy was, in turn, to be advised by a mostly Indian Executive Council.
  - The electorate was increased to 36 million adults; 30 per cent of the population.
- The Act went almost as far as it could go without granting complete Home Rule.
- Both Congress and the Muslim League criticised the Act:
  - Congress rejected the special protection of minorities and the proposed weak central government.
  - Jinnah called it 'totally unacceptable' because he believed it failed to give Muslims any real power in a new Indian government.

The 1937 elections and their impact on Congress / Muslim League relations

- Eventually both the Muslim League and Congress (now led by Jawaharlal Nehru) agreed to take part in the forthcoming elections with the intention of disrupting the political process.
- Out of a total of 1585 seats, Congress won 715.
- Considering the scale of their victory (they won control of eight out of the eleven provinces) they decided not to disrupt the government but instead use it to their advantage:
  - Political prisoners were released.
  - Civil rights were restored, for example freedom of speech.
  - Loans were provided to help farmers modernise.
  - Compulsory primary education was introduced.
- Congress now demanded a more powerful central government that reduced the power of the provinces. The Muslim League was outraged.
- Congress and the Muslim League became more divided and many Muslims, including Jinnah, left Congress in protest. Gandhi's call for Hindi to become India's official language was seen as the last straw.
- Support among Muslims for the Muslim League increased again when it began to campaign for a completely separate Muslim state called Pakistan.

Summary Box 2

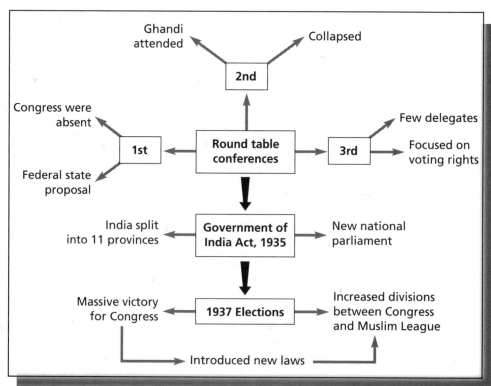

Key Topic

8 India during the Second World War

The impact of the Second World War on India

- Viceroy Lord Linlithgow declared war on Germany in September 1939, without consulting a single Indian and thereby ignoring the 1935 Government of India Act.
- Congress politicians resigned in protest from all levels of government.
- Jinnah angered Congress by immediately declaring a 'Day of Thanksgiving' to celebrate Congress' withdrawal from politics.
- The Muslim League supported the war and exploited the absence of Congress from Indian politics.
- In March 1940 the Muslim League made its 'Lahore Declaration', the first public call for a separate Muslim state. It was to be called 'Pakistan' meaning 'Land of the Pure'.
- The Lahore Declaration angered Congress but made the Muslim League far more popular among Muslims. Between 1937 and 1945 the percentage of Muslims who voted for the Muslim League rose from 5 per cent to 90 per cent.
- In October 1941, Gandhi launched a new civil disobedience campaign, hoping to force the British to grant immediate independence to India.

The Cripps Mission

- At the beginning of 1942 the British feared a Japanese attack on India through Burma. The British desperately wanted full Indian support for the war.
- In March 1942 Sir Stafford Cripps was sent to India to seek an agreement with India's leading parties.
- Cripps offered:
  - Total independence at the end of the war.
  - An all-Indian Executive Council with much greater power.
  - Freedom to leave the Commonwealth at the end of the war.
  - Any province which did not want to be part of the new India would be allowed to become independent.
- Cripps' offer was rejected by Congress. It wanted immediate control over the Executive Council, with all power and decisions made by Indians.
- The British government rejected these demands.

Gandhi's 'Quit India' Campaign, August 1942

- Despite the constant fear of Japanese attack, Gandhi called for a 'Quit India' campaign and demanded that the British leave India immediately.
- Gandhi encouraged non-violent protests which led to the closure of shops, businesses, markets and ports as Indians marched in protest against British rule.

- In spite of Gandhi's call for non-violent action, rioting did break out all over India, directed against both the British and Muslims.
- The Muslim League condemned Gandhi and Congress as traitors, whilst Jinnah believed the Quit India campaign was 'blackmailing the British and coercing them to establish a Hindu Raj'.
- Viceroy Linlithgow ordered the immediate arrest of Congress leaders and activists.
- The arrests sparked violent outbreaks. 1000 died and 100,000 were arrested in the months that followed. As a result Congress was effectively silenced throughout India.
- Despite the large number of marches and picketing, industrial production and volunteers for the Indian army continued to rise.
- By the end of 1942 the Quit India campaign had died out.

Bose and the Indian National Army (INA)

- Subhas Chandra Bose had left Congress because he opposed Gandhi's non-violent methods. He began to use more militant tactics against the British:
  - Bose was smuggled into occupied Singapore by the Japanese army. He recruited a 20,000 strong 'Indian National Army' (INA) from Indian army prisoners of war and deserters.
  - In 1943 he declared himself the head of the 'Provisional Government of Free India' and attempted to destroy British rule using terrorist attacks.

What do I Know?

1 How many Round Table conferences took place?
2 In which years?
3 What was the main aim of these conferences?
4 When was the Second Government of India Act introduced?
5 How many seats did Congress win in the 1937 elections?
6 What did the Lahore Declaration call for?
7 What was the main aim of the Cripps mission?
8 Who organised the 'Quit India' campaign?
9 Who was Subhas Chandra Bose?

My score ....

▲ Jinnah

▲ Gandhi

▲ Nehru

▲ Chandra Bose

▲ Mountbatten

- ○ Railway stations and junctions, isolated army units, police stations and communication lines were sporadically attacked over a period of 18 months.
- ○ The INA never really threatened British rule, mainly because the Indian army remained extremely loyal throughout the war.
- ○ In 1945 Bose was killed in a plane crash as he attempted to escape to the Soviet Union.

Key Topic

9 The post-war search for a solution

The Simla Conference (June – July 1945)

- When Viceroy Wavell took office he released Gandhi and all the Congress leaders from prison.
- Wavell proposed:
  - ○ The creation of a new all-Indian Executive Council.
  - ○ The formation of new provincial and national assemblies.
  - ○ A fixed number of seats for Muslims, Sikhs and other minority groups in every Indian assembly and on the Executive Council.
- The conference collapsed because Congress and the Muslim League demanded to select the Muslims who would sit on the reserved seats.
- Congress and the Muslim League were at loggerheads.

The Cabinet Mission (April 1946)

- In July 1945, just as the Simla Conference collapsed, a new Labour government was elected in Britain led by Clement Attlee.
- Attlee sent an eight-man Cabinet Mission to India, led by Sir Pethick Lawrence, in the spring of 1946.
- On 16 May the Cabinet Mission published its proposals:
  - ○ Immediate dominion status.
  - ○ Full independence at the earliest opportunity.
  - ○ A three tier federation:
    - ○ This gave central government powers over foreign policy and defence and national communication networks.
    - ○ Provincial governments formed the second tier of government by taking control of local by-laws, police, education, health and public works schemes.
    - ○ Individual provinces would be permitted to join together. They might choose to agree common policies across several provinces and therefore form a third tier of government.
- Congress and the Muslim League welcomed the proposals.
- On 7 July, Nehru told a Congress meeting that Congress was not bound by the proposals and might reject them in the future.
- Jinnah and the Muslim League interpreted this as a major U-turn and believed they could no longer trust Congress.
- When, on 22 July 1946, Wavell invited Congress and the Muslim League to form an interim government in preparation for independence, the Muslim League also did a U-turn and rejected the Cabinet proposals.

Direct Action

- Nehru's own U-turn on the Cabinet Mission's proposals destroyed what little faith the Muslim League had left in Congress. From this point, the Muslim League became determined to form the separate state of Pakistan.
- On 16 August 1946 Jinnah declared a 'Direct Action' campaign against Congress and British rule. He called on Muslims to begin a **hartal**.
- Whatever Jinnah's aims, violence erupted in Sind, Bengal and Calcutta, where 15,000 people died in just three days.
- By September 1946 supporters of the Muslim League had begun terrorist attacks on police officers, communication networks and the army.
- When, on 2 September 1946, Nehru became India's first prime minister, not a single Muslim League representative turned up to Nehru's first government meeting.
- The Cabinet Mission, once surrounded with great optimism, had proven to be a failure.

Hartal
The closure of all businesses and shops.

Key Topic

10 The end of British rule: The birth of two new states

Viceroy Lord Louis Mountbatten

- By February 1947 India was in chaos and virtually ungovernable. Wavell retired and was replaced by Mountbatten. He was the last viceroy of India.
- Mountbatten announced the British government's 'definite intention' to hand over full power no later than June 1948.
- A date was then fixed for independence. The British would leave at midnight on 28 August 1947.
- At first Mountbatten hoped to keep India united, but soon abandoned this hope after witnessing first hand the terrible violence on the streets.
- Gandhi had by now become determined to halt the violence at all costs. He even urged Congress to allow Jinnah to rule any future India, rather than it being partitioned.
- When Congress rejected this proposal Gandhi retired from politics and spent the rest of his life encouraging peace and harmony between Hindus and Muslims.
- On 3 June 1947 Mountbatten officially proposed:
  - The creation of two separate states; India and Pakistan.
  - All princely states to choose whether to join Pakistan or India, or to remain independent.
- Both Congress and the Muslim League accepted the proposal.
- Mountbatten set the date of partition and independence for 14 August 1947.
- Each individual provincial assembly was given the power to decide which country to join.
- All provinces except Sind, Baluchistan, North West Frontier Province, West Punjab and East Bengal joined India.

- All the princely states, except Junagadh and Hyderabad, opted to join India. Nevertheless the Indian army was ordered by Nehru to invade both princely states and force them to become part of India.
- Kashmir was invaded by both Indian and Pakistani forces. Both countries have argued over this area since 1947.

The birth of Pakistan and India

- India became independent on 15 August 1947.
- Mountbatten became governor-general of both Pakistan and India. This was a ceremonial and temporary position whilst both countries prepared for full independence.
- Jinnah described the birth of Pakistan and India as being 'drowned in blood'.
  - Between June and August 1947 a mass migration of Hindu and Muslim people between Pakistan and India took place.
  - 6 million Hindus moved from Pakistan to India.
  - 5 million Muslims moved from India to Pakistan.
  - The movement of refugees led to widespread violence and many people were killed as they attempted to escape.
  - 600,000 people died in the Punjab alone.
- On 30 January 1948, just as Gandhi was planning a visit to Pakistan, he was shot three times in the chest. Gandhi's assassin was a Hindu extremist who opposed Gandhi's attempts to bring peace and harmony between the Hindu and Muslim communities. A national radio statement read, 'Mahatma Gandhi was assassinated in New Delhi at twenty past five this afternoon. His assassin was a Hindu.' The last sentence saved India and Pakistan from further massacres and atrocities.
- The entire world was united in its mourning for Gandhi.

Of Gandhi's death Albert Einstein said,

Generations to come will scarce believe that such a man as this, in flesh and blood, ever walked upon this earth.

and Nehru declared,

The light has gone out of our lives and there is darkness everywhere.

Summary Box 3

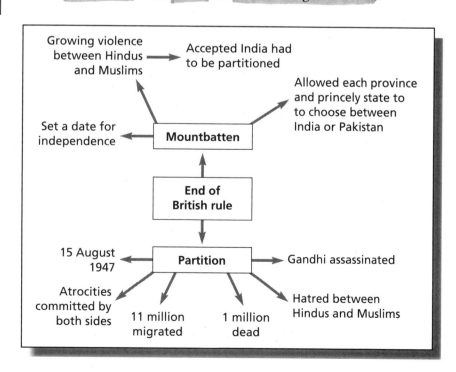

**What do
I Know?**

1 When did the Cabinet Mission make its proposals?
2 List its main proposals.
3 When did Jinnah declare 'Direct Action'?
4 What is 'hartal'?
5 How did some people interpret 'Direct Action'?
6 What date did the British government fix for Indian independence?
7 What did Mountbatten propose on 3 June 1947?
8 When did independence actually take place for India and Pakistan?
9 Over which area have India and Pakistan argued (and fought) since 1947?
10 When was Gandhi assassinated?

My score ....

**Exam Type
Questions**

A typical **Section A** question:
1 What was meant by the 'swadeshi campaign'?   **(3)**

Answer 1

'Swadeshi' means 'of our own country' and began after Lord Curzon tried to divide Bengal in half in 1905. It was a way of getting the British to listen to India's demands.

**Examiner's
Comments on:
Answer 1**

2 out of 3
The candidate correctly identified the origin of the campaign and meaning of 'swadeshi'. However they failed to identify the nature of the campaign; for example there was a boycott of the purchase or sale of foreign goods.

A typical **Section B** question:
2 Explain why demands for Indian independence grew in the years between 1900 and 1919.   **(10)**

Answer 2

Between 1900 and 1919 the British made a series of mistakes that increasingly angered the Indian people and encouraged them to unite against British rule.

When Lord Curzon tried to divide Bengal in 1905, Congress successfully organised a national swadeshi campaign in protest. This turned Congress from a small and unknown party into India's main opposition group. The swadeshi campaign united Indians against British rule for the first time and reminded them of their own power.

The Morley-Minto Reforms of 1909 gave a small group of Indians a say in how India should be governed. Although Indians were not given any powers to create new laws, it was seen as a step in the right direction and proof that a carefully planned national campaign could force the British to introduce reforms.

During the First World War most Indians loyally served the British war effort. They hoped it would lead to the reward of Home Rule at the end of the war. When Lord Montagu made his famous Declaration in August 1917, it indeed seemed India was about to be awarded dominion status like New Zealand or Canada. However, when the war ended Montagu was forced to go back on his promises and introduce the unpopular Government of India Act (1919) known as the Montagu-Chelmsford Reforms. This gave Indians greater control of local areas, but the national government remained firmly in the hands of the British. The Indian people felt let down and betrayed by the British – as though the 62,000 Indians who died in the war had done so in vain.

Then in 1919 the British made two even bigger mistakes. The first was the Rowlatt Act which removed an Indian's right to free speech and a fair trial. Then in April 1919 the horrific Amritsar Massacre finally put the last nail in the coffin of British rule. This was because Brigadier Dyer had acted so cruelly and the British refused to punish him in any way – in fact he was widely praised! After Amritsar the Indian people were united and determined to shake off British control.

During this period India's communication network became more modernised. This allowed Congress leaders to travel throughout India drumming up support and meant that stories of massacres could be easily told throughout the entire country. In the past India's size and remoteness helped the British isolate opposition – this was no longer possible by 1919.

Examiner's Comments on: Answer 2

9 out of 10

This is a very chronological study of the period between 1900 and 1919. This can be a useful way of covering all the key information. The candidate wisely avoids describing each event or reform in detail. Instead the candidate explores how each event or reform affected Indian public opinion. The answer ends with an interesting theory that communication networks may have contributed to the growth of opposition to British rule.

9. The USA: A divided union? 1941–80

As a result of the Second World War the USA finally escaped the Great Depression and became the most powerful and wealthy country on Earth. Whilst US soldiers fought for the principle of freedom, sections of US society remained powerless and poverty stricken. Throughout the period 1941 to 1980 these disadvantaged groups, like black people and women, used various methods to achieve equality and recognition within the USA.

What do I Need to Know?

You need to be aware of the key issues in US post-war history, including that its society appeared divided, often to the point of violence or death, the impact of the Second World War and how lives were destroyed by the fear of communism. In addition, you need to understand how black, female and young Americans felt like second-class citizens.

Key Topics

1 What was the impact of the Second World War on the US economy and government?

The economy

- The war proved to be a good thing for the US economy.
  - 17 million new jobs were created and unemployment was wiped out.
  - Wages increased by 30 per cent.
  - By Christmas 1942 US industrial output was greater than Japan, Germany and Italy's combined.
  - In 1945 the USA was producing more iron and steel than the entire world had produced in 1939.
  - Industrial production trebled.
  - The number of jobs rose by 52 per cent.

The government

- The job of the US President was originally meant to be to look after any issues that affected the 50 states which made up the USA. This usually meant that presidents only became important during wars.
- However, following the First World War (1914–18) and the Great Depression (1930s) the US people began to accept that the country would benefit from laws and regulations that were common across all 50 states. These were called 'federal laws'.

- During the Second World War this move towards federal rather than state laws and regulations increased.
- By the end of the Second World War most Americans believed that the country would do better if the power of the federal government were to be increased at the expense of state governments.
- This vast increase in presidential and federal power became very important in the civil rights era and the Vietnam War.

Summary Box 1

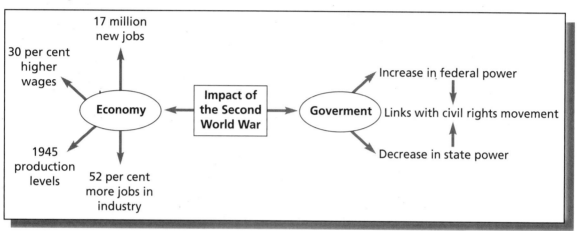

Key Topic

2 What was the impact of the Second World War on US society?

Women

- **Propaganda** images such as 'Rosie the Riveter' symbolised the way in which many women were forced to adapt to new factory roles.
  - By 1945, one-third of all industrial workers were women, as opposed to one-quarter before the war. There were 18 million female workers in industry by 1945.
  - Over 350,000 women had served in the army, 80,000 of whom worked overseas as nurses, interpreters and clerics.
  - Women had various organisations they could join. 200,000 joined the Women's Army Corps (WACs) or the Navy's Women Appointed for Voluntary Emergency Services (WAVES). Many joined the American Red Cross.
  - 6 million women worked in war production factories.
  - Women worked as machinists, ship builders, crane operators, toolmakers, railtrack layers and welders.
- Facory work meant higher pay for women but not equal pay. Women still endured the sexist attitudes of men and tended to leave their jobs soon after the end of the Second World War.

- Some women resented losing the independence that a salary had given them.

Black Americans

- Before the Second World War, black Americans were often treated as second-class citizens. However, the war again acted as a catalyst for change.
  - Over 1 million black people joined the army, but there was segregation in the armed forces too.
  - Only 12 black officers were appointed. Black soldiers were rarely allowed to fly or navigate planes, or even to be sent into combat.
  - Black people were often given jobs in kitchens and living quarters and were not allowed to provide blood for transfusions.
  - Black women could join the armed forces as nurses, but could only tend to black soldiers.
- As the war progressed, the situation improved:
  - There was an increase in the number of black officers and pilots.
  - Black soldiers saw combat duty.
  - Black people were allowed to give their blood for transfusions.
- Mixed race combat units were formed, for example, at the Battle of the Bulge in late 1944.
- Black leaders like Philip Randolph saw the war as an ideal opportunity to improve the lives of black Americans:
  - He and others created the 'Double V' campaign that sought victory abroad and at home.
  - Randolph organised a 100,000 strong mixed race march on Washington in late 1941, aiming to draw public attention towards the plight of black Americans.

Discrimination

Treating someone differently because of their skin colour, religion, age or gender.

- Roosevelt feared strikes among black people and their sympathisers and appeased them with the creation of the Fair Employment Practices Committee (FEPC). The FEPC investigated racial **discrimination** and prevented large companies from winning war production contracts unless they eradicated racism within their companies.
- Above all, the Second World War raised black and national consciousness about the situation in the USA. The National Association for the Advancement of Coloured People (NAACP) attracted almost 0.5 million members by 1945 and made racial equality the most important domestic issue for the first time in 100 years.

Migrate

To move home, either abroad or from one part of a country to another.

- By 1944 over 2 million blacks had **migrated** north to work in war industries. The arrival of so many black Americans created racial tensions in some cities.
- Racial tension rose gradually throughout the war and actually resulted in a series of riots. In Harlem (New York), for example, 300 people were injured and six blacks died.

Japanese Americans

- Shortly after the Japanese attack on Pearl Harbor, President Roosevelt authorised the internment (arrest without trial) of over 100,000 Japanese Americans, nicknamed 'enemy aliens'.
- The government feared they would become agents for the Japanese government, acting as spies, saboteurs and traitors.
- Japanese Americans were taken from their homes and sent to relocation camps. They had $0.5 billion worth of property and possessions confiscated or forcibly sold on their behalf.

Summary Box 2

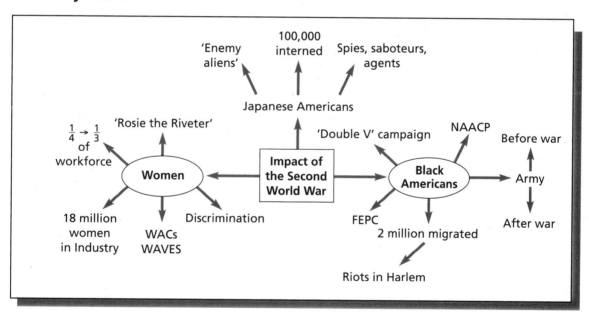

What do I Know?

1 What effect did the war have on the US economy?
2 Who was 'Rosie the Riveter'?
3 How many female industrial workers were there in 1945?
4 What was the 'Double V' campaign?
5 What was FEPC?
6 How many Japanese-Americans were arrested after the attack on Pearl Harbor?

My score ....

Key Topic

3 Why had the USA developed a fear of communism by 1950?

- **1945:** The USA now occupied the western half of Europe: the Soviet Union occupied the eastern half. Both sides feared a further advance by the other.
- **1946:** Winston Churchill described this division as an 'Iron Curtain', and confirmed that the wartime alliance was well and truly dead.
- **1947:** President Truman approved the 'Federal Employee Loyalty Programme' (FELP). This vetted and sacked anyone suspected of being a communist and other 'traitors'.
- **1947:** The **Senate's** 'House of Un-American Activities Committee' (HUAAC) investigated communist infiltration in all walks of life, especially Hollywood. Potential superstars were 'blacklisted' by actors such as Ronald Reagan, who acted as informers. The 'Red Scare' had begun.
- **1948:** The Soviet Union unsuccessfully blockaded West Berlin and appeared to be planning an attack on western Europe.
- **1948:** Alger Hiss, a former official of the US State Department (who might have had access to defence and foreign policy documents), was falsely accused of copying and passing documents to the Soviet Union. Despite a lack of evidence he spent five years in jail.
- **1949:** Communists took power in China. The Soviet Union exploded its first atom bomb.
- **1950:** Communist North Korea invaded democratic South Korea. Two scientists, Julius and Ethel Rosenberg, were convicted of passing nuclear secrets to the Soviet Union during the Second World War. Both were executed in 1953. In their defence they said they passed secrets to an ally of the USA, not an enemy.
- **1950:** Senator Joseph McCarthy began to stir up US anti-communist fears.

Senate

America's 'upper house', similar to the British House of Lords. Each state has two senators.

Summary Box 3

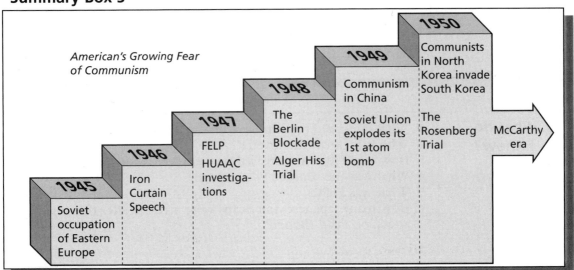

American's Growing Fear of Communism

1945 Soviet occupation of Eastern Europe

1946 Iron Curtain Speech

1947 FELP HUAAC investigations

1948 The Berlin Blockade Alger Hiss Trial

1949 Communism in China Soviet Union explodes its 1st atom bomb

1950 Communists in North Korea invade South Korea The Rosenberg Trial

McCarthy era

Key Topic

4 The McCarthy Era

What happened?

- In 1950 McCarthy claimed to have a list of 205 members of the Communist Party working in the State Department. (He was lying but nobody could prove it.)

- At first no one, not even President Truman, dared challenge him, out of fear that he would label them a communist as well.

- McCarthy forced 2375 innocent people to appear before the Senate's House of Un-American Activities Committee to explain their activities, including Walt Disney.

- No-one was safe from McCarthy's accusations. Although he never produced any evidence, many public figures had their reputations ruined and 400 ended up in jail.

- It was not just those who ended up in court that suffered. Being suspected of being a communist could result in an American being 'blacklisted' and thereafter struggling to find a decent job.

Why did 'McCarthyism' end?

- By 1954 the tide had finally turned against McCarthy.

- Once McCarthy's interrogations were televised the public turned against his rude, aggressive manner and demanded to see the evidence he failed to show.

- In a last bid for credibility McCarthy claimed that the US army was infiltrated with communists. This was the last straw; he was now insulting a source of US pride and honour.

- McCarthy's popularity began to decline. He was **censured** by the US Senate in 1954 for 'improper conduct'. He died in 1957.

- Relations with the Soviet Union had been improving since the death of Stalin in 1953.

Censured

Official word in politics to describe heavy criticism and condemnation.

What was the impact of McCarthyism?

- 9500 civil servants were sacked, 15,000 resigned, 600 teachers were forced out of their jobs and many actors, writers and performers saw their careers ruined, for example, Charlie Chaplin. Many even committed suicide.

- The 1954 'Communist Control Act' banned the Communist Party in the USA.

- The McCarthy affair showed how fearful the USA was of communism and the 'Red Scare'.

- As late as 1960, some US states still demanded an oath of loyalty from their employees.

Summary Box 4

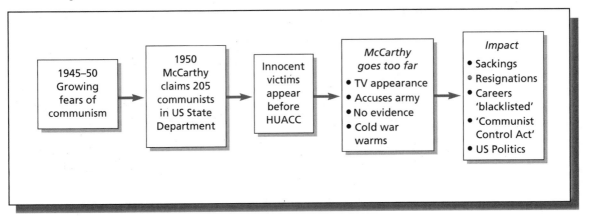

| 1945–50 Growing fears of communism | → | 1950 McCarthy claims 205 communists in US State Department | → | Innocent victims appear before HUACC | → | *McCarthy goes too far* • TV appearance • Accuses army • No evidence • Cold war warms | → | *Impact* • Sackings • Resignations • Careers 'blacklisted' • 'Communist Control Act' • US Politics |

What do I Know?

1 What was the HUAAC?
2 What was the 'Red Scare'?
3 What was Alger Hiss accused of?
4 How many people did McCarthy claim to have on his list of communists?
5 How did McCarthy's allegations affect people in public life?
6 Give two reasons why McCarthyism ended.

Key Topic

5 The Civil Rights Movement

The condition of black American lives in the 1950s

American Constitution

A mixture of laws and rights dating back to 1776. Since this time many changes or additions have been made.

- Despite the 13th, 14th and 15th Amendments to the **American Constitution** (which abolished slavery, and granted citizenship and voting rights for all), individual states were able to implement their own segregation laws that made these federal laws useless.

- These racist state laws were nicknamed 'Jim Crow Laws'.

- In the southern racist states their 'Jim Crow Laws' ensured that:

  ○ Black people struggled to gain voting rights through literacy requirements and intimidation.

  ○ Schools for black people were of a weaker standard.

  ○ Black hospitals and clinics were understaffed and poorly supplied.

  ○ Schools, parks, swimming pools, water fountains, public transport, shops and benches were segregated.

- The US government conducted its own investigation into poverty and found that 18 per cent of all white Americans lived below the poverty line. This compared to 56 per cent of all black Americans.

- Millions of black Americans had not yet enjoyed the prosperity of the post-war USA.

The Civil Rights Movement part one: Truman

- Truman had recognised the need for the USA to do something about black rights.
- He successfully forced the army to integrate fully by 1950, and demanded that military contracts continue to be awarded to non-racist companies in peacetime.
- Unfortunately he was unable to introduce a civil rights bill aimed at ending **lynching** and guaranteeing voting rights for black Americans.

> **Lynching**
>
> Unlawful executions usually carried out by racist gangs.

The Civil Rights Movement part two: The 1954 Brown v Topeka Board of Education Decision

- With the assistance of the NAACP, the parents of eight-year-old Linda Brown sued the town of Topeka for preventing their daughter from attending the nearby school which was an all-white school.
- On 17 May 1954, the US Supreme Court declared that schools in the USA could not be segregated.
- This was a key moment because it was the first attempt in 100 years by the federal government to outlaw segregation by overriding state laws.
- Black people all over the USA gained confidence in the court's decision and became more determined to gain freedom and equality.
- Despite this federal ruling, six states continued to disobey the court's decision. It was not until 1964 that schools were forcibly desegrated.

The Civil Rights Movement part three: The Montgomery Bus Boycott, 1955

- On 1 December 1955, Rosa Parks refused to give up her seat on a bus to a white man. She was arrested, but refused to pay her $14 fine.
- Within two days Martin Luther King organised a one-year boycott of buses that attracted worldwide attention and public sympathy.
- In December 1956 the US Supreme Court declared that segregation on buses was illegal.

The Civil Rights Movement part four: Little Rock High School, 1957

- In September 1957, nine black students were due to begin their studies at Little Rock High School, in the state of Arkansas. The Governor of Arkansas, Orval Faubus, sent thousands of National Guardsmen to stop the black students entering the school.
- Once the federal government declared this illegal, the Guards were withdrawn and the black students were left to defend themselves against a white mob.
- President Eisenhower sent in 10,000 federal troops to protect the students throughout the rest of the school year.
- In September 1958 Faubus unsuccessfully tried to close all schools in Arkansas, unless the government agreed to end its ban on segregated schools.
- The US Supreme Court declared segregated schools illegal and ordered the reopening of all schools on a non-segregation basis. It was not until 1964 that all schools obeyed the decision.

The Civil Rights Movement part five: The Kennedy years

- Kennedy became US President in 1960 and was keen to bring about improvements for black Americans.
- In 1961, white and black youths called 'Freedom Riders' travelled on southern buses and trains, in an attempt to enforce Supreme Court rulings.
  - Despite enormous intimidation, violence and occasional murders, these 'Freedom Riders' again encouraged public sympathy and maintained civil rights as the key political issue in the USA.
- In 1963 the city authorities in Birmingham, Alabama, attempted to reverse decisions made on desegregation. Parks, swimming pools and other public places were closed to avoid integrating them. As a result Martin Luther King organised a series of marches and demonstrations in Birmingham.
  - Martin Luther King and 3500 other peaceful protesters (including children) were mauled by police dogs and arrested on the order of the local police commissioner, Eugene 'Bull' Connor.
  - TV cameras filmed what was going on. Americans were outraged and disgusted that their own police force could treat peaceful protestors in such a brutal and vicious manner.
  - As a result, Kennedy submitted his Civil Rights Bill to Congress in June 1963.
  - Martin Luther King organised a huge civil rights march on Washington in 1963.
- Black unity and determination was symbolised by Martin Luther King's famous 'I have a dream' speech about a future free from racial prejudice, made during this march on 28 August 1963.

- More than 250,000 people (including 80,000 white Americans) listened to the speech, which earned Martin Luther King the Nobel Peace Prize in December 1964.

The Civil Rights Movement part six: In Kennedy's memory

- Kennedy was assassinated in November 1963 before his Civil Rights package could be passed.
- Kennedy's successor, Lyndon B Johnson, took up Kennedy's proposals for improved civil rights.

The successes of the Civil Rights Movement

- The Civil Rights Act of 1964 outlawed racial discrimination and segregation in all walks of American life.
- The Equal Employment Opportunity Commission was created to deal with complaints.
- The Voting Rights Act of 1965 outlawed minimum literacy and wealth levels from being a bar to voting.
- In 1967 the Supreme Court ruled that state laws which criminalised interracial marriages were illegal.
- In 1968 the Civil Rights Act was extended to outlaw unfair distribution of welfare housing.
- Eventually, the growing dominance of the war in Vietnam shifted public attention away from Martin Luther King and his calls for even greater equality.

The failures of the Civil Rights Movement

- The Civil Rights Movement revived violent and racist groups like the Ku Klux Klan (KKK).
- In the late 1960s race riots broke out all over the USA. In the first nine months of 1967 more than 150 US cities reported racially motivated violent disorders.
- Even by 1966 most blacks lived below the poverty line. In 1966 a black American baby was twice as likely to die before the age of five compared with a white baby.
- The Civil Rights Movement and Martin Luther King became increasingly unpopular among sections of the black community, who believed Martin Luther King's methods were too cowardly and produced few real benefits.
- Malcolm X is the best known member of the Black Muslims. They believed in using force to get equal rights.
- Other people such as Stokely Carmichael believed in 'Black Power'. He believed that black people should take control of their lives and be separate from white society.

Summary Box 5

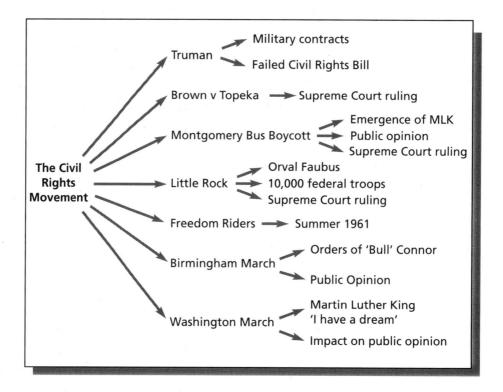

The Civil Rights Movement

- Truman
  - Military contracts
  - Failed Civil Rights Bill
- Brown v Topeka → Supreme Court ruling
- Montgomery Bus Boycott
  - Emergence of MLK
  - Public opinion
  - Supreme Court ruling
- Little Rock
  - Orval Faubus
  - 10,000 federal troops
  - Supreme Court ruling
- Freedom Riders → Summer 1961
- Birmingham March
  - Orders of 'Bull' Connor
  - Public Opinion
- Washington March
  - Martin Luther King 'I have a dream'
  - Impact on public opinion

Key Topic

Inaugural address

The first speech made by a new US president.

6 Kennedy's 'New Frontier'

- The 'New Frontier' Policy was announced by Kennedy in his **inaugural address** in January 1961.

- In his address (or speech) Kennedy vowed to create economic growth, improve public programmes, defeat discrimination and 'get the country moving again'.

How did he try to do this?

- He increased the minimum wage to $1.25 and gave extra money to the poorest states, such as Kentucky, to tackle long term poverty.

- He also tried to introduce two bills; the 1961 Medical Care for the Aged Bill and the 1961 Education Bill. Both failed to get through Congress.

- His greatest triumphs were the Housing Act (this provided huge sums of money to begin renewing urban slums) and the Manpower Development and Training Act (this provided $900 million to retrain and relocate thousands of unemployed industrial workers).

- He proposed a tax cut in 1963 which he hoped would lead to a growth in spending and an increased demand for goods.

- In June 1963, Kennedy tried to introduce a comprehensive 'Civil Rights Bill'. This would ban discrimination in employment, and ensure equal voting rights and equal access to housing and education.

Why did Kennedy find it difficult to carry out his 'New Frontier' Policy?

- Congress was against him. There were various reasons for this:
  - Kennedy failed to get the Republicans or conservative Democrats to support him. He relied on support from the southern states who saw him as too radical and unduly sympathetic to minorities.
  - Kennedy promoted lots of young people (e.g. William Manchester) to top jobs and lots of black people (e.g. Robert Weaver). This annoyed the older, white politicians.
  - Congress was worried about Kennedy's spending plans on education and the elderly. Most did not like the idea of the government taking responsibility for people's needs; it had not in the past, and the USA was used to '**laissez faire government**'. Some described these new plans as 'communism'.

Laissez faire government
The belief that an economy is more effective if left unregulated and uncontrolled by the government.

Summary Box 6

Kennedy's New Frontier

PROBLEMS	SOLUTIONS	BARRIERS
POVERTY	• Minimum wage • Medical Care for the Aged Bill • Education Bill	(1) Failed to win over conservative southern Democrats and Republicans
COMMUNISM	• Increased arms spending • Troops sent to Vietnam	(2) Fears over his spending plans (3) Seen as too radical
DISCRIMINATION	• Introduced Civil Rights Bill	

What do I Know?

1 What was the nickname given to racist state laws?
2 What does the term 'segregation' mean?
3 Give two examples of segregation.
4 What did the Supreme Court decide on 17 May 1954?
5 Which event sparked off the boycott of buses in 1955?
6 What took place on 28 August 1963?
7 What were the aims of Kennedy's 'New Frontier'?

My score ....

7 Johnson's 'Great Society'

- This was Johnson's dream to eradicate poverty and discrimination across the USA.

- Despite its initial successes, US money and attention became increasingly diverted by the war in Vietnam.

What were the successes of Johnson's 'Great Society'?

- Between 1964 and 1966 there were some key successes:
  - **1964:** the Civil Rights Act.
  - **1965:** Medical Care Act (for the elderly and those dependent on welfare).
  - **1965:** Voting Rights Act (ended literacy and property tests before voting).
  - **1966:** Model Cities Acts (funded slum clearance).
  - **1966:** Minimum wage increase from $1.25 to $1.40.

- By late 1966 the war in Vietnam had become the central priority and money dried up for welfare programmes. Johnson dropped his plans for 'zero poverty within 10 years'.

- From 1967 onwards, constant demonstrations and riots across the USA ended the optimistic **honeymoon period** Johnson had enjoyed following Kennedy's death.

> **Honeymoon period**
> A short period of time following the election of a new leader when the media temporarily minimises criticism.

Summary Box 7

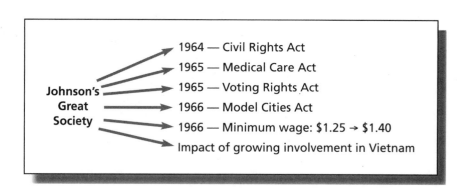

Johnson's Great Society
- 1964 — Civil Rights Act
- 1965 — Medical Care Act
- 1965 — Voting Rights Act
- 1966 — Model Cities Act
- 1966 — Minimum wage: $1.25 → $1.40
- Impact of growing involvement in Vietnam

Key Topic

8 The War in Vietnam

- This was the USA's longest and most costly war, and the first one it lost.

- US involvement in Vietnam stretched over a period of 19 years (1956–75) under four different presidents (Eisenhower, Kennedy, Johnson and Nixon).

130

- Worldwide media exposed the horrors of modern warfare and the treatment of the Vietnamese by US soldiers.

- Public opinion began to shift, especially among US youth.

- By 1969, 48 per cent of Americans expressed opposition to the war in Vietnam. Parents were horrified that their children might become soldiers and die in a foreign land.

- Thousands of students became 'draft dodgers' by going into hiding or studying abroad. Still more became 'drop outs and bums', opting instead for an alternative, anti-establishment lifestyle: the hippy age.

- Anti–war protests occurred all over the USA. Many of them turned violent. For example, four students were killed at Kent State University in 1970. Americans had become divided and opposed to one another over the issue of the Vietnam War.

- The war in Vietnam cost 58,156 US lives, 400,000 Vietnamese lives, $141 billion and created 5 million Vietnamese refugees.

Summary Box 8

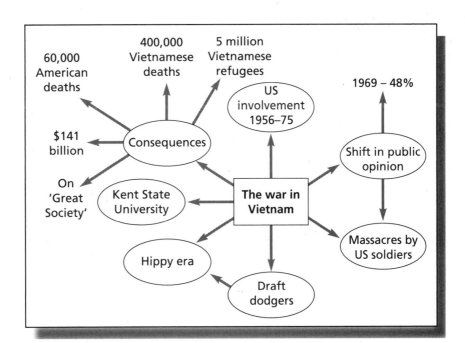

What do I Know?

1 What was President Johnson's 'Great Society'?
2 List two successes of the 'Great Society'.
3 Why was Johnson unable to complete his dream of a 'Great Society'?
4 What is a 'draft dodger'?

My score ....

9 Popular protest movements

The Women's Movement	*The Student Movement*
• Fuelled by Betty Friedan's book *The Feminine Mystique* in 1963 and the introduction of the contraceptive pill in 1960. Both encouraged and enabled greater independence and freedom among women. • The women's movement was based on their sense of injustice. Women were stereotyped in the media as housewives. • More men were at college and men were in higher paid professional jobs. • There were virtually no prominent women in politics. The most famous was Jackie Kennedy, who was admired for her appearance, not her political intellect. • Women were paid less for the same job as men and women were not entitled to maternity benefits. • The civil rights movement grew to include the equal treatment and payment of women as well as black people: **1961:** Kennedy set up the Presidential Commission on the Status of Women and began investigating equality. **1963:** Equal Pay Act. **1964:** Civil Rights Act: employment could not be determined on the grounds of gender or race. **1966:** NOW (National Organisation for Women) was set up. They campaigned and coordinated action for women's equality. **1972:** Educational Amendment Act combatted the stereotyping of women in textbooks and examinations. • Gradually more jobs became open to women and the pay gap narrowed, but opportunities and numbers in politics have still not equalised.	• This developed for a variety of reasons, but it was mainly due to the war in Vietnam. • Students wanted to avoid the 'draft' (conscription). They felt the war was immoral and imperialistic. They didn't want to die fighting for something they saw as wrong. • Most considered their government to be corrupt and unfair. They wanted a greater say in how their education was run. They set up the SDS, Students for a Democratic Society. • They also had a number of other anxieties against censorship, nuclear weapons, racism and capitalism. • Their feelings culminated in hundreds of peaceful anti-war demonstrations. One ended in tragedy at Kent State University (Ohio) in 1970, when four students were shot dead by National Guardsmen. • A distinctive music culture accompanied the movement, for example, The Doors, Janis Joplin, Simon and Garfunkel and, especially, Bob Dylan. • Young people developed an alternative lifestyle that was a reaction to their parents' and society's expectations. These people were known as 'hippies' and became associated with Flower Power, marijuana, LSD, free love, vegetarianism, and their anti-war stance. Their slogan was 'make love, not war'. • Finally, there was widespread pessimism created by the deaths of JF Kennedy, Malcolm X, Martin Luther King and RF Kennedy. They were all heroes who seemed to be challenging the traditional establishment.

The Black Power Movement

- The Black Power Movement grew as a response to the perceived failure of Martin Luther King's non-violent protest.

The Nation of Islam/Black Muslims

- Elijah Muhammad led this radical group. Elijah believed that his predecessor, Wallace Fard, was Allah and that he was therefore a disciple of god.
- The Nation of Islam believed that whites were evil and therefore blacks should not live or work alongside white people.
- They wanted segregated communities where whites and blacks could run their own affairs without the other's involvement.
- Unlike Martin Luther King, the Nation of Islam encouraged blacks to use violence as a means of forcing change and encouraged blacks to convert from Christianity (known as 'the white man's religion') to Islam, along with abandoning their 'Christian slave name'.
- One such American changed his name from 'Cassius Clay' to 'Mohammed Ali'.
- By the mid 1960s the Nation of Islam began to split and prominent members, like Malcolm X, openly criticised Elijah and formed their own groups.

Black Panthers

- This group was not as segregational as the Nation of Islam but saw total integration as impossible for many centuries.
- They wanted blacks to dominate local business, politics, education and welfare rather than rely on whites' goodwill.
- All wanted equality but were divided over the methods that could be used and whether blacks and whites could live happily together.

▲ **Women's lib demonstration in New York City, August 1970.**

▲ **US students protest against the Vietnam War, May 1970.**

▲ **Elijah Muhammad reads at the National meeting of Black Muslims, August 1966. Mohammed Ali also appears (right).**

Summary Box 9

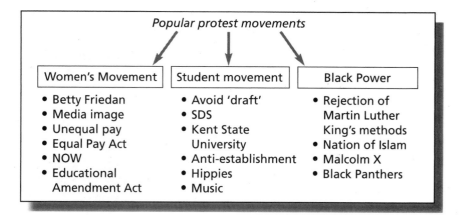

Popular protest movements

Women's Movement	Student movement	Black Power
• Betty Friedan	• Avoid 'draft'	• Rejection of
• Media image	• SDS	Martin Luther
• Unequal pay	• Kent State	King's methods
• Equal Pay Act	University	• Nation of Islam
• NOW	• Anti-establishment	• Malcolm X
• Educational	• Hippies	• Black Panthers
Amendment Act	• Music	

Key Topic

10 The Watergate Scandal

An outline of the Watergate Scandal

- **17 June 1972:** Five burglars were caught trying to break into rooms rented by the Democratic Party presidential election team in the Watergate building in Washington DC. All five were members of Nixon's CREEP (Campaign to Re-Elect The President). CREEP hoped to discover information about the Democratic Party's election strategies.
- **August 1972:** Nixon denied any involvement in the burglary but secretly ordered nearly $500,000 to be given to the burglars in return for their silence.
- **7 November 1972:** Nixon won a landslide presidential election, the second biggest in history.
- **May 1973:** One of the burglars, John McCord, feared a long prison sentence and admitted that some 'White House staff' were involved in the burglary, but not Nixon himself.
- Two of Nixon's closest advisors were forced to resign.
- One of these advisors, John Dean, then admitted to a Senate investigation that although Nixon had no part in planning the burglary he had tried to cover up the scandal afterwards. Dean also revealed that Nixon had secretly tape-recorded all conversations within the White House and the truth could be found on those reels.
- **July 1973:** The Senate **subpoenaed** Nixon's secret tapes. After a long refusal Nixon finally started to hand over sections of the tapes, from November 1973 onwards.
- The tapes destroyed Nixon. He appeared to be foul mouthed, aggressive, sexist and racist.
- The Senate finally threatened to **impeach** Nixon. Rather than face a long prison sentence Nixon resigned on 7 August 1974.
- The tapes proved that Nixon had tried to use the CIA to block an FBI investigation into the burglary.
- Nixon's pledge to the US people in the 1972 election that 'there can be no whitewash at the White House' was proven to be a false promise.

subpoena

to summon to court.

impeach

to charge a public official in court with misconduct in office.

- **8 August 1974:** Gerald Ford became the next President and one month later pardoned Nixon and therefore closed the matter.

The impact of the Watergate Scandal

- Nixon was forced to resign and was replaced by his Vice-President, Gerald Ford. An angry Congress reduced presidential powers. The War Powers Act meant that Congress had to approve any future declaration of war.
- There were much tighter controls on presidential spending. Nixon, for example, had authorised the spending of $500,000 from the nation's defence budget on a security system for his private ranch in California. It turned out that the security system was a golf course!
- The Privacy Act was passed. This allowed people access to any files the government may have gathered on them. Public respect for politicians declined considerably.
- Gerald Ford lost the 1976 presidential election and was replaced by Jimmy Carter, a Democrat.
- In 1976 the USA celebrated the bicentenary of their country's birth amidst an atmosphere of presidential scandal and military defeat. The USA appeared more divided than ever before.

Summary Box 10

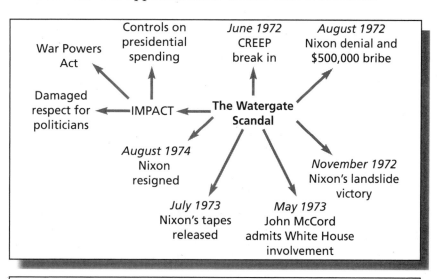

What do I Know?

1 Which two factors helped fuel the women's movement in the 1960s?
2 Give examples of the unequal treatment of US men and women in the 1960s.
3 What were 'hippies'?
4 Name two black protest groups.
5 Which organisation were the burglars who broke into the Watergate building members of?
6 Why did Nixon resign?
7 Who succeeded Nixon as president?

My score ....

Exam Type Questions

A typical **Section A** Question:
1   What was meant by Jim Crow Laws?   (3)

Answer 1

These were racist laws against black people in the USA. Not all states used them, only those in the 'Deep South' like Mississippi and Alabama.

Examiner's Comments on: Answer 1

2 out of 3
The candidate clearly understands the racist nature of the Jim Crow Laws and that they were only found in certain states across the USA. However the candidate fails to give examples of these laws, for example, segregated water fountains or public transport. The failure to give examples is a very common error in these low mark questions.

A typical **Section B** question:
2   What was the impact of the Second World War on the USA?   (15)

Answer 2

The war made the USA the richest and most powerful country on Earth. Millions of new jobs were created, especially for black Americans and women. Also US factories were producing more weapons than everyone else was. This meant that the US victory was inevitable. It was only a matter of time before the USA would win.

The USA entered the war on 8 December 1941 after the Japanese airforce bombed Pearl Harbor. For some reason Hitler also declared war on the USA on the 11 December 1941. Therefore the USA had to fight a war against Germany as well. US soldiers had to fight in Europe, Asia, and North Africa. Therefore it really was a world war. Nearly half a million Americans died in the war.

The US army invaded Nazi occupied France on 6 June 1944, called D-Day. After nearly one year Hitler killed himself and the Germans finally surrendered. Then the USA concentrated on Japan and beat them as well after they dropped two atom bombs on Hiroshima and Nagasaki.

> After the war the USA and the Soviet Union became superpowers and ruled everyone else. The USA became the policeman of the world and was also the richest country in the world as well.

Examiner's Comments on: Answer 2

5 out of 15

This candidate has a good basic knowledge of the war. Although the candidate touches on some of the key consequences of the war they do not do so in sufficient depth. In other words, what effects did the war have on the US people and their government?

Ideally there should be attention given to the economy, the government, black Americans, women and Japanese Americans, ending with a conclusion that might examine whether the USA was a better place in 1945 compared with 1941.

Practice Questions

1. What is meant by 'Black Power'? **(6)**
2. How successful were presidents Kennedy and Johnson in fighting poverty and discrimination? **(15)**

10. The rise and fall of the communist state: The Soviet Union, 1928–91

Topic Summary

Between 1928 and 1991 the Soviet Union rose from being a backward agricultural nation to a strong superpower. Tens of millions of workers and soldiers died during this transition, either as a result of war or through government policies. By 1991 this powerful superpower had collapsed and with it the communist rule that had begun in 1917. Ordinary Soviet people suffered greatly during these years, from famine, fear, war and shortages.

What do I Need to Know?

You will need to know how each key leader of the Soviet Union attempted to modernise or adapt the country's government, agriculture and industry between 1928 and 1991. In addition you will need to address how successful Stalin, Khrushchev and Gorbachev were during their time in power. In particular you will need to be aware of how the Soviet people were affected throughout this period and by the Second World War.

Key Topics

1 Stalin's rise to power

- Joseph Stalin worked his way up through the ranks of the Bolshevik Party after he joined at the age of 22.
- Stalin gained the respect of Lenin because of his loyalty and devotion to the party.
- In 1922 he became the General Secretary of the Communist Party. He used this position to ensure the appointment of his own supporters to the Communist Party and the removal of the older party members whose loyalty he could not depend upon.
- Following Lenin's death in 1924, Stalin jointly led the Soviet Union with Trotsky, Kamenev and Zinoviev. By 1928 Stalin had discredited these rivals and established himself as the sole leader of the Soviet Union.
- Throughout the 1930s Stalin successfully strengthened his position as leader of the Communist Party (and therefore the Soviet Union) and established a powerful dictatorship until his death in March 1953.

Summary Box 1

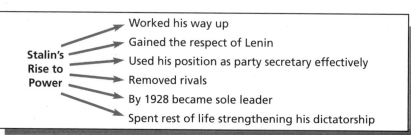

Stalin's Rise to Power
- Worked his way up
- Gained the respect of Lenin
- Used his position as party secretary effectively
- Removed rivals
- By 1928 became sole leader
- Spent rest of life strengthening his dictatorship

Key Topic

2 Stalin's changes in industry

Why did Stalin believe that changes were necessary?

- Stalin was convinced that the backward state of Soviet industry would condemn its people to continued poverty and defeat in war.
- He believed that the future of both communism and the Soviet Union would only be secure if the Soviet Union was industrialised and modernised in just ten years. Stalin said in 1931:

We are 50 to 100 years behind the advanced countries. We must catch up this distance in ten years. Either we do this or we go under.

- In 1928 Soviet industry was very old fashioned and unproductive. US factories were on average ten times bigger than Soviet factories.

What were the Five-Year Plans?

- Stalin began his changes in industry in 1928 when he announced the first Five-Year Plan. The Five-Year Plans had a number of elements:

  - Fear was used to encourage workers: Stalin's secret police (the NKVD) were always ready to remove slow workers, poor managers, slackers, doubters or **saboteurs**.

  - Individual production targets were set for each factory, mine, quarry and construction site.

  - Volunteers from the *Komsomol* (youth movement) worked in factories.

  - Enormous public works programmes built essential infrastructure, for example the Dnieper Dam, the Belomor Canal, the widening of the Trans-Siberian railway and the Moscow underground system. These programmes often used *zeks* (prisoners from labour camps, or *gulags*).

  - Propaganda campaigns were used to encourage workers to make better efforts, for example the Stakhanov movement (named after Alexi Stakhanov, a coal miner who cut 102 tonnes of coal in a shift compared to the usual 7 tonnes).

  - Local factories, mines and quarries were set targets by **Gosplan**.

  - All workers were retrained by Shock Brigades, copying US production methods.

  - New industrial centres were built in remote areas of the Soviet Union, such as Magnitogorsk, Stalinsk and Karaganda.

Saboteurs

People who deliberately damage or destroy tools or machinery.

Gosplan

The USSR's state planning authority under Stalin.

- The Five-Year Plans often did not last five years because Stalin usually claimed their targets had been achieved in less time. Each Five-Year Plan changed its focus to suit the needs of the economy:

1st Five-Year Plan 1928–32	2nd Five-Year Plan 1933–7	3rd Five-Year Plan* 1938–41
Oil	Oil	Oil
Coal	Coal	Coal
Iron	Iron	Iron
Steel	Steel	Steel
	Tractors	Tractors
	Electricity	Electricity
	Military	Household goods
		Military

* cut short by the Nazi invasion of the Soviet Union

How successful was industrialisation?

The successes

- The Red Army was transformed into the biggest army in the world, with modern armaments.
- Public works schemes improved the Soviet Union's **infrastructure**.
- New cities like Magnitogorsk began exploiting the Soviet Union's raw materials.
- Education programmes transformed the Soviet Union. Moscow University became the biggest in the world, free education was introduced from age 4 to 11, and there were literacy and numeracy programmes for industrial and agricultural workers.
- The production of all major industrial materials rose significantly between 1928 and 1940. Oil production rose by 300 per cent, coal and iron by 400 per cent, steel by 500 per cent and electricity by 700 per cent. Overall the amount of industrial production rose by 400 per cent.
- The Soviet Union's industrial production was greater than Britain's, similar to Nazi Germany's, and only beaten by that of the USA.

The failures

- The human cost: estimates range from 10 to 40 million deaths as a direct result of Stalin's plans for modernisation.
- The cities became very overcrowded and food was in short supply, especially during the winter of 1932–3.
- Production focused on heavy industry and the military. Very little was made that might improve Soviet people's quality of life, for example, household goods or clothing.
- Production figures were very unreliable: workers, managers, Gosplan and Stalin all lied and exaggerated these figures to make them look more impressive.

> **Infrastructure**
>
> A country's road, rail and communications network.

- Workers' lives became difficult. Food was in short supply, fear of being arrested and deported to a gulag by the NKVD was ever present, free movement was restricted by passports and harsh rules existed, for example, you could be executed for accidentally breaking a tool or a machine.
- The quality of Soviet goods was often very poor, for example, half of all tractors built in 1934 had broken down by 1935. Between 1928 and 1937, 40 per cent of all manufactured goods were declared faulty.

Summary Box 2

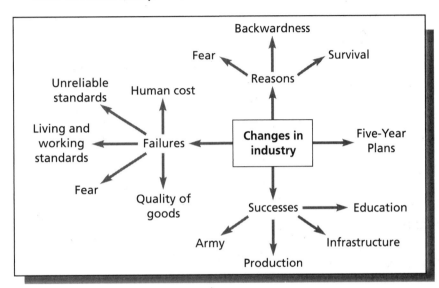

What do I Know?

1 When did Stalin emerge as the leader of the Soviet Union?
2 What was the state of Soviet industry in 1928?
3 How many Five-Year Plans were there?
4 List the key focuses and dates of the Five-Year Plans.
5 Why was the final Five-Year Plan interrupted?
6 Give two successes and two failures of the Five-Year Plans.
7 Who was Alexi Stakhanov?

My score ....

Key Topic

3 Stalin's changes to agriculture

Why did Stalin want to introduce changes?

- Most Soviet farms were small, **subsistence** farms and very inefficient.
- Agricultural production was a fraction of that being achieved in other countries such as Germany, Britain and the USA.
- Since Lenin introduced the New Economic Policy in 1921 most farms were privately owned and therefore out of Stalin's control. Stalin labelled owners of these farms as 'kulaks'. He wished to destroy the kulaks so that he could control all farming himself.

Subsistence farm

A farm where food is not produced for sale, but for private consumption.

- Stalin needed more industrial workers to work in the cities so he wanted machines to replace peasants in the countryside, for example, tractors and combine harvesters.

What changes did Stalin introduce?

- Stalin wanted to group together all smaller farms into enormous collective farms called *kolkhoz*. These farms would be state managed and controlled.
- Collective farmers would be set production targets. Farmers were only allowed to keep produce once they had achieved their targets.
- In theory, all collective farms were to have their own schools, hospitals, agricultural training, homes and a Motor Tractor Station, where free machinery and tools could be kept for the benefit of everyone on the collective farm. In practice, very few of these were available.
- At first Stalin tried to convince all peasants to join, but few were interested. Then Stalin ordered the enforced collectivisation of the Soviet countryside and declared war on the **kulaks**.

What was de-kulakisation?

- Stalin declared,

  We must smash the kulaks, eliminate them as a class. We must strike at the kulaks so hard that they will never rise to their feet again.

- Red Army soldiers and NKVD squads were sent into the countryside for two reasons. Firstly to requisition (confiscate) food, and secondly to force peasants to leave their farms and move into the industrial centres. Those who resisted were rounded up and sent to labour camps (gulags), or forced to work in factories. Many were shot in their own homes defending their property.
- Rather than give up all they had worked for, many peasants decided to eat, burn and destroy all that they owned. Over half the livestock and harvests in the Soviet Union were destroyed in the summer and autumn of 1932.
- The result was a horrific famine in 1932–3. Approximately 20 million people died as a direct result of this famine.
- Stalin continued to sell grain abroad during this period.
- Stalin himself admitted that up to 10 million peasants suffered at the hands of the Red Army and NKVD. Most disappeared to gulags or their corpses were thrown from trains as they headed to Siberia.

What were the successes of collectivisation?

- By 1940, 99 per cent of all land was part of a collective farm.
- By 1940 agricultural production was beginning to exceed 1928 levels.

Kulaks

Wealthy peasants who had come to own a small plot of land following Lenin's New Economic Policy of 1921.

- New modern techniques and chemicals were introduced for the first time.
- Subsistence farming was replaced by performance-related pay.
- Stalin was now able to control the supply of food into the Soviet Union's cities.
- Since 1933 the Soviet Union has never experienced another famine, the longest period in its history.

What were the failures of collectivisation?

- Agricultural production by 1940 was barely higher than in the days of Tsar Nicholas II.
- Production was still much less efficient than in other developed countries.
- Approximately 10 million peasants' lives were ruined by deportation to gulags or industrial centres.
- The Great Famine of 1932–3 resulted in the death of 10 million Soviet people, both farmers and city workers.

Summary Box 3

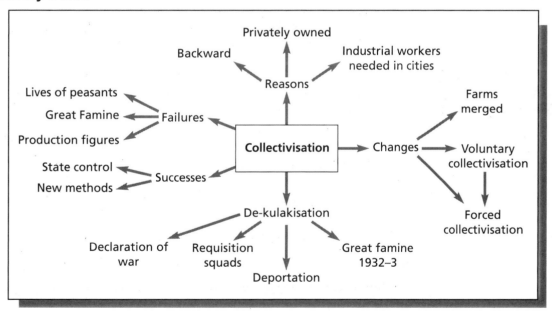

Key Topic

4 What was it like to live in the Soviet Union in the 1930s?

- Soviet peasants experienced starvation, deportation, armed threats or relocation to one of the Soviet Union's industrial centres.
- There were benefits for Soviet workers: education and healthcare were both improved, whilst the average life expectancy actually went up in the 1930s.

- Soviet women were granted full equality with men. Industrial work was increasingly dominated by women (especially during the Second World War), whilst education and healthcare were seen as women's professions. Over 60 per cent of Soviet doctors were women by 1940.
- Better housing, rations and holidays were available for hardworking industrial workers. Very few managed to achieve the 'Stakhanov Standards' let alone receive extra benefits.
- However, there was a much darker side to the 1930s. Workers constantly lived in fear of being labelled a slacker, doubter, wrecker, spy or saboteur.
- The NKVD drove round at night in dark vans nicknamed Black Ravens, rounding up all those who had been accused of crimes. This era of **the purges** was perhaps the darkest hour in the Soviet Union's history.
- The law did not protect ordinary workers or peasants. People settled disputes or old rivalries by making up false accusations against neighbours. Husbands informed on wives, children informed on parents. Everyone lived under the constant threat of arrest and deportation.
- During the 1930s, Soviet cities became even more overcrowded and squalid. There was an increase in crime, alcoholism and suicide. Food prices rose faster than wages whilst top Communist Party bosses enjoyed the luxury and privileges that the tsarist nobility had once enjoyed.

The Purges

The name for Stalin's campaign against his supposed enemies.

Summary Box 4

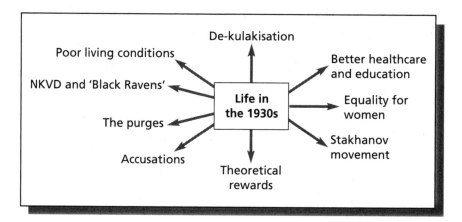

What do I Know?

1 What was a *kolkhoz*?
2 What was a kulak?
3 In what years did the Soviet Union experience a famine?
4 What happened to the people who resisted collectivisation?
5 Which benefits came to Soviet women in the 1930s?

My score ....

Key Topic

5 The nature of Stalin's dictatorship

How was Stalin able to secure himself as an absolute dictator?

- **Purges:** Up to 40 million people were purged between 1934 and 1953. This included anyone perceived to be a threat to Stalin's authority or his police, e.g. kulaks, political opponents such as Trotsky, industrial workers, poets, artists, scientists, managers and leading military personnel.

- **Gulags:** These labour camps (similar to Nazi concentration camps) provided a cheap labour force to carry out enormous public works schemes. There were 12 million **zeks** by 1939; their average life expectancy in a gulag was just two years.

- **Secret police force:** Stalin used the NKVD to spy on and round up any political opponents or ordinary workers (similar to Hitler's SS or Gestapo). The NKVD was led by Yagoda, then Yezhov and finally Beria, all of whom were subsequently executed. NKVD agents were even sent to Mexico to hunt down and kill Leon Trotsky in 1940.

- **Show trials:** These were public trials of former leading communist politicians where people 'confessed' to crimes they had not committed. They were used to justify the extent of Stalin's purges and eliminate rivals, for example Kamenev, Bukharin, and allies of Trotsky and Zinoviev.

- **Education:** A new national curriculum was written to ensure that Stalin's version of history and the Bolsheviks' rise to power was accepted across the Soviet Union. Stalin's close relationship with Lenin was exaggerated; rivals like Trotsky were literally rubbed out of photographs, and other evidence that might threaten Stalin's authority was destroyed.

- **Cult of Personality:** Education, the arts and newspapers were used to encourage the worship of Stalin as a demi-god. He was portrayed as the father of all Soviet people.

- **Censorship:** All art and literature was banned if it challenged or questioned Stalin's character or policies.

- **Propaganda:** Soviet films, books, posters and radio broadcasts exaggerated or invented achievements under Stalin. In addition, all forms of art were to follow 'Socialist Realist' principles aimed at glorifying the achievements of the Soviet Union and Stalin.

What was the impact of the purges?

- Virtually every walk of life in the Soviet Union was affected by the purges.

Zeks

Russian word for a labour camp prisoner.

Top Communist Party leaders:

- By 1940, of the 24 members of the Central Committee of the Bolshevik Party of 1917:
  - 8 had been executed (including Kamenev, Bukharin, Zinoviev and Trotsky).
  - 7 had mysteriously 'disappeared'.
  - 7 had died 'naturally' (including Lenin).
  - 1 was in prison.
  - 1 was alive and well – Stalin!

The armed forces:

  - All admirals were executed.
  - Most marshals were executed.
  - Many army commanders were executed.
  - Most members of the Supreme Military Council were executed.
  - Between 18,000 and 35,000 officers were executed.

The security services:

  - Yagoda (head of the NKVD) was executed following a show trial.
  - Yezhov (Yagoda's successor) was executed.

Others:

  - 12 million Kulaks had died.
  - 1 million implicated in Kirov's murder had been killed.
  - 5 million ethnic minorities (including Chechens and Latvians) had been killed.
  - 10 million returning prisoners of war had died.
  - 1 million assorted 'political criminals' had been sent to gulags; over half of them died.

Total number of victims = 35–40 million

Conclusions

- The purges allowed Stalin to create a climate of fear that forced people to work hard and demonstrate their loyalty.
- The millions who were sent to gulags worked on huge public works schemes so the purges had some economic advantages.
- Industry suffered because managers were too scared to try new innovations.
- The arts were stifled as only works that portrayed Socialist Realism were allowed.
- The purges within the armed forces weakened the Soviet Union and led to defeats at the beginning of the *Great Patriotic War* of 1941–5 (the Soviet term for their involvement in the Second World War).
- However, Stalin was able to create an extremely loyal army as a result of the purges.

Summary Box 5

Key Topic

6 The impact of the Second World War on the Soviet Union

What were the key events of the Second World War?

- 23 August 1939: Nazi-Soviet Non-Aggression Pact: Stalin and Hitler agreed never to go to war with one another.
- 22 June 1941: Operation Barbarossa: Germany attacked the Soviet Union. Initially this was very successful with gains of 80 km (50 miles) per day; within eight hours two-thirds of the Soviet airforce was destroyed. Then the intensely cold weather slowed down the German advance.
- August 1941: The Germans reached Leningrad and besieged the city until January 1944. 600–900,000 Leningrad civilians were killed.
- September 1941: Over the next four months, 80 per cent of Soviet industry was dismantled and transported eastwards behind the Ural mountains. Artillery left behind was deliberately destroyed to avoid it being used by the Germans. This was known as the 'scorched earth policy'.
- August 1942: The Germans encircled Stalingrad. Fighting took place. By February 1943 the Sixth German army was forced to retreat and was encircled by Red Army troops led by General Zhukov and Nikita Khrushchev.
- July 1943: The Battle of Kursk: the biggest tank battle in history was won by the Red Army. Germany's defeat now seemed certain.
- April 1945: The Red Army encircled Berlin.
- 8 May 1945: Following Hitler's suicide a week earlier, the German army unconditionally surrendered.

What was the social impact of the Second World War?

- 28 million Soviet people died; most were civilians.
- 600–900,000 of these died in Leningrad alone.
- Deaths were brought on by starvation, hypothermia and German air attacks.
- 25 million people were made homeless, partly as a result of German bombing but also due to the 'scorched earth policy'.
- Over 3 million Soviet citizens were deported to Siberia, in case they sided with the Germans.
- Women dominated industrial and agricultural production.

What was the political impact?

- Despite the early military disasters, Stalin's purge of the armed forces meant that the Red Army was never in danger of surrender or mutiny.
- A fierce propaganda campaign depicted Stalin as the genius who had masterminded victory against the Germans.
- At the end of the war Stalin was more popular, and more secure in power, than ever before.
- Despite an alliance with the USA, after 1945 the Soviet Union and USA entered into a Cold War.

What was the economic impact of the Second World War?

- A third of all industry was destroyed.
- Nearly half of all farmland was destroyed.
- 5 million homes and thousands of towns and farms were destroyed.
- By 1944, the Soviet Union was producing more industrial goods than in 1941. Most industry was situated behind the Ural mountains and was operated by women.

Summary Box 6

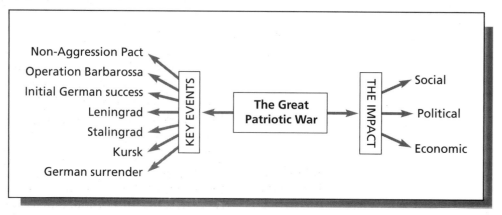

**What do
I Know?**

> 1 What were the purges?
> 2 When was Trotsky killed?
> 3 What were the show trials?
> 4 What was the Cult of Personality?
> 5 Approximately how many people were killed during the purges?
> 6 In which year did Germany first attack the Soviet Union?
> 7 What was the 'scorched earth policy'?
> 8 Which Soviet city suffered particularly badly during the war?
>
> **My score** ....

Key Topic

7 Khrushchev and de-Stalinisation

What do we know about Stalin's death?

- Stalin died on 5 March 1953 as a result of a stroke.
- He left behind:
  - A country that had not fully recovered from the Second World War.
  - An enormous and powerful secret police force (led by Beria).
  - A potentially catastrophic Cold War with the USA.
- It was unclear who would succeed Stalin. There were four serious contenders: Beria, Khrushchev, Molotov and, the favourite, Malenkov.
- By December 1953 Beria had been executed for plotting to illegally gain control of the Soviet Union.
- In little over two years, Nikita Khrushchev managed to secure the leadership of the Soviet Union. This was achieved through his support among the armed forces and the popularity he enjoyed following his 'secret speech'.

What was the 'secret speech'?

- In February 1956 Khrushchev made a speech to the Twentieth Communist Party Congress.
- His speech was an attack on Stalin's personality and his years in power. It was the first time that anyone had publicly attacked Stalin for over 25 years.

> Stalin invented the idea of an 'enemy of the people'. He used this to carry out the most cruel actions against anybody whom he suspected. The facts show that many abuses were carried out on Stalin's orders. He paid no attention to either the rules of the Communist Party or the laws of the Soviet Union. Stalin's behaviour not only affected life in the Soviet Union, but also our relations with foreign countries.
>
> (Khrushchev, February 1956)

- The speech denounced Stalin as a cruel dictator who had selfishly used the purges to rid the Soviet Union of personal enemies and innocent victims. Khrushchev claimed that Stalin had illegally abused his power, breaking not only the laws of the Communist Party but also those of the Soviet Union. Finally, Khrushchev appeared to be trying to improve relations with the USA.
- The following day Stalin's body was removed from its resting-place next to Lenin and buried unceremoniously next to the Kremlin Wall.
- Khrushchev's speech was greeted enthusiastically by both ordinary Soviet people and by people in the West.
- The speech gave Soviet people the impression that Khrushchev had nothing to do with Stalin's oppression. Also, the other two contenders for the leadership of the Soviet Union were immediately associated with Stalin's cruelty because they had failed to make a similar speech.

What was de-Stalinisation?

- Stalin's burial was the first in a long line of decisions aimed at destroying Stalin's reputation, or Cult of Personality.
- Stalingrad was renamed Volgograd.
- Paintings and photographs were altered so that Stalin's image did not appear next to Lenin's.
- School textbooks were re-written to give slightly more accurate accounts of the 1917 Revolution.
- Posters, statues and monuments of Stalin were removed.
- The secret police force (the NKVD) was radically reformed. Its leader, Beria, was executed and replaced by a committee. Khrushchev hoped this would prevent the secret police being used for personal reasons, as Beria had done. Finally, it was renamed the KGB.
- Thousands of *zeks* were released from the gulags and given official pardons. (Although they were not allowed to leave the adjoining towns.)
- Millions of ethnic minorities who had been deported during the Second World War were allowed to return home.
- Censorship laws were relaxed and new artistic styles and books were permitted. Books such as Boris Pasternak's *Dr Zhivago* or Alexander Solzhenitzen's *A Day in the Life of Ivan Denisovich,* which actually made criticisms of the Soviet system, were published. Solzhenitzen's book in particular gave an account of life in the gulags. It was a step in the right direction, but censorship was only relaxed – not abolished.
- Ordinary Soviet people understood the secret speech to be permission to criticise all aspects of the Soviet rule, including Khrushchev himself.

- By 1961 Khrushchev was forced to reintroduce the death penalty because of the growing climate of criticism throughout the Soviet Union.
- The impact of the speech was also felt in other countries. People in Poland and Hungary believed it was a sign that the Soviet Union would no longer insist on communist governments in their country. As a result, thousands of Polish and Hungarian rebels rose up against their communist leaders. Hungarians in particular suffered as a result of Khrushchev's orders to send in the Red Army and execute rebel leaders.

Summary Box 7

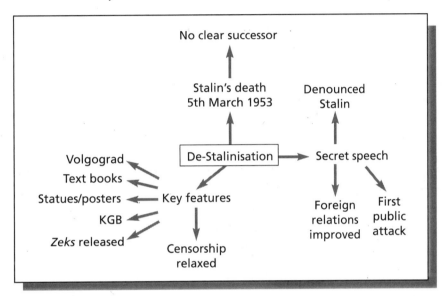

Key Topic

8 Khrushchev's attempts at modernisation

How did Khrushchev try to reform agriculture?

- Khrushchev considered himself to be an expert in agricultural matters.
- Despite being the biggest country on Earth, covering one-sixth of the world's land, the Soviet Union was still struggling to feed its own people: Khrushchev aimed to solve this problem using three methods:
  1 **The Virgin Lands Scheme**: An area the size of France would be farmed for the first time in Kazakhstan/western Siberia. It was hoped that over 20 million tonnes of extra grain would be harvested.
  2 **The amalgamation and reform of the collective farms**: Thousands of collective farms were to be joined together to form bigger and more efficient farms. Farmers' debts were to be written off and much higher prices paid for their produce.
  3 **The introduction of maize**: Khrushchev gave incentives for farmers to grow maize as a substitute for traditional animal fodder. He hoped that this would mean more grain would be released for human consumption.

What were Khrushchev's industrial reforms?

- Khrushchev's agricultural reforms allowed farmers greater control over their decision making. Khrushchev hoped this would act as an incentive and that production would increase. This move towards greater independence and less central control was also mirrored in industrial reforms.
- Rather than everything being controlled in Moscow by state planning authorities like Gosplan, Khrushchev divided the country into 100 regional economic councils called *sovnarkhozys*. These regional councils were allowed to make independent decisions based on what was right for that particular area.
- As a result controls on workers were relaxed, performance-related pay was introduced and factories began to work along the lines seen in capitalist countries.
- Khrushchev famously remarked, 'What sort of communism is it that cannot produce a sausage?' He realised that the Soviet Union had to produce much more food and consumer goods.
- Khrushchev ordered factories to produce more luxury goods which would increase the standard of living.
- To prove the achievements of communism, Khrushchev was determined that the Soviet Union should win the **space race**.

> **Space race**
>
> The race between the USSR and the USA to develop space technology.

What were the consequences of Khrushchev's policies?

- Khrushchev became very unpopular among ordinary Soviet people and within the Communist Party itself. But did Khrushchev really deserve that much criticism?

Yes:

- Maize was often grown in unsuitable soil. This meant valuable land was wasted on crops that would never grow.
- Inexperienced but enthusiastic young communists (the *Komsomol*) ran the Virgin Lands Scheme. Their inexperience led to soil being over-farmed and exhausted. In 1963 hurricanes swept most of the topsoil away and left the ground completely useless for farming. Canadian and Australian grain was bought at high prices to avoid famine.
- The Soviet rail network was so undeveloped in Kazhakstan that useful grain rotted because there were not enough trains to transport it to the cities.
- The increased wages to farmers doubled their standard of living (temporarily) but the Soviet Union was unable to afford it.
- In the cities local factory managers were used to being told what to do under Stalin and were unable to cope with their new-found independence. The result was confusion, errors and increased unhappiness among the workers.
- The space race achievements were spectacular but they failed to produce any real benefits for ordinary Soviet people.

'Whilst Gagarin orbited the earth we counted on abacuses.'

[A Russian housewife speaking in 1990.]

No:

○ Grain harvests rose sharply the years between 1953 and 1964. Despite the great winds of 1963, the Soviet Union recorded its highest ever grain harvest in 1964.

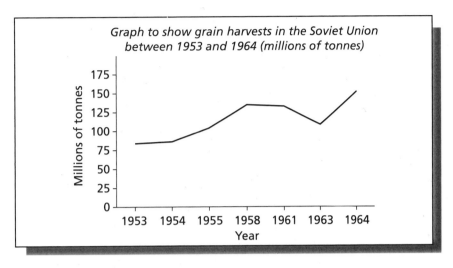

Graph to show grain harvests in the Soviet Union between 1953 and 1964 (millions of tonnes)

○ Khrushchev had at least tried to tackle the lack of initiative and ambition that Stalin had stifled when he was in power.
○ Ownership of luxury goods rose dramatically (although it was many years behind the West). The goods were usually of poor quality and did not provide valuable exports.

Luxury goods ownership, 1955 and 1966.
(The figures are the number of goods per 1000 people.)

		1955	1966
Cars	A typical Soviet citizen would need to save their entire wages for 7 years before they could afford a car. Most became scrap after just 3 years.	2	5
TVs	All TV programmes were heavily censored and promoted Khrushchev and communism.	4	82
Refrigerators	Designers were encouraged to reduce the size of refrigerators so that they would not appear so empty.	4	40
Washing machines	In a bid to meet targets, some factory workers used nails instead of rivets to hold washing machines together.	1	77

○ The Soviet people were proud of their space race achievements. Up to 1969, the Soviet Union was always ahead in the space race. They were first to send a satellite, dog, man, woman and space station into space.

Khrushchev's fall from power

- By 1964 Khrushchev was becoming very unpopular.
- Prices had risen by 30 per cent (wages had not), the death penalty had been restored, a famine had been narrowly avoided by purchasing foreign grain, factories and collective farms had their independence reduced, and the Soviet Union appeared to have backed down in the Cuban Missile Crisis.
- Other Communist Party leaders were embarrassed by Khrushchev's rude and uncouth behaviour.
- In October 1964 Khrushchev was forced to retire and was succeeded by Leonid Brezhnev.
- A number of years later Khrushchev stated:

The most important thing I did was just this … that they were able to get rid of me simply by voting, whereas Stalin would have had them all arrested.

Summary Box 8

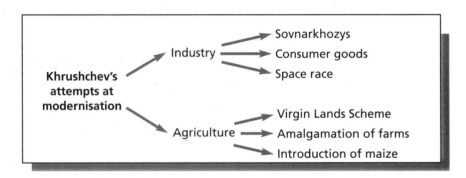

What do I Know?

1 When did Stalin die?
2 Who replaced him as leader of the Soviet Union?
3 When did Khrushchev make his secret speech?
4 Define 'de-Stalinisation'.
5 List three ways in which Khrushchev reformed agriculture.
6 What are *sovnarkhozys*?
7 Who replaced Khrushchev as leader?

My score ………

Key Topic

9 Gorbachev's attempts at reform

What problems did Gorbachev face in 1985?

- Mikhail Gorbachev came to power in 1985. He was young, friendly, liberal and well educated. The West greeted this new leader with much hope and less suspicion than other leaders. However, he faced a number of enormous problems.

- *Political problems*
  - The Soviet Union had experienced four leaders (Brezhnev, Andropov, Chernenko, Gorbachev) in just four years. The country was not used to such instability.
  - Under Brezhnev (1964–82) the number of dissidents (opponents) had massively increased; many were placed in mental hospitals.
  - Top Communist Party leaders' families were corrupt. Brezhnev's daughter and son-in-law, for example, were involved in fraud and corruption.
  - Stalin's generation of communist bosses was dying out and a new wave of younger, more **liberal** men began to outnumber the old guard. This new core was in favour of sweeping reforms.

Liberal

Open minded and moderate in outlook.

- *Economic problems*
  - The Soviet economy was virtually bankrupt. Top Communist Party officials and their families were abusing and exploiting the economy for their own gain.
  - Soviet industry was increasingly backward and old-fashioned, unable to keep up with developments like the microchip and electronic revolutions.
  - The Soviet Union's military commitments in eastern Europe and its costly nuclear weapons were becoming impossible to maintain.
  - Luxury goods were scarce or unaffordable. A car cost seven years' wages and usually broke down within a few years.
  - Queuing became a normal part of everyday life; most turned to the black market instead.
  - In 1981 Brezhnev stated in a speech to top Communist Party leaders that the reasons for the country's failures were:

    lack of skilled labour, alcoholism, absenteeism, and lack of effort on the part of civil servants who manned the vast organisation which tried to plan the economy.

- *Social problems*
  - Brezhnev's statement indicates the enormous problems that existed for Soviet workers.
  - By 1980 the Soviet Union had the highest alcoholism rate in the world, crippling absenteeism and the most unproductive workforce in Europe.
  - Workers' homes were basic and simple. There were few opportunities to escape the vicious cycle of life that communism had brought.

- *Military problems*
  - By 1985, the Soviet Union's bankruptcy could be blamed on its military commitments both in and outside its borders.

○ Since the Second World War the Soviet Union had controlled much of eastern Europe, fearing a western attack.

○ Since Christmas 1979 the Soviet Union had been fighting a costly war against Afghanistan.

○ The **Arms Race** with the USA was crippling the Soviet economy. Weapons were becoming reliant on high technology (for example, the 'Strategic Defence Initiative').

○ The 1985 Chernobyl nuclear disaster underlined the enormous legacy of the arms race and the Cold War.

How did Gorbachev try to solve these problems?

- Gorbachev had five main aims:

1 End the Cold War with the USA. This would reduce the military budget and hopefully improve the Soviet economy.

2 Pull the Red Army out of Afghanistan.

3 End the Soviet Union's commitment in eastern Europe; again, this would help reduce the military budget.

4 **GLASNOST**: meaning 'openness'. Gorbachev wanted the Soviet Union to appear open and friendly with the West, rather than treat it with suspicion and fear. Gorbachev hoped that this new image would encourage foreign **investment** and new technology.

5 **PERESTROIKA**: meaning 'economic restructuring'. Gorbachev wanted to end Moscow's central planning and introduce some elements of capitalism. For example, allowing factories to set their own targets, prices and wages. Gorbachev wanted to encourage enterprise and competition, the basis of successful western economies.

> **Arms race**
>
> The race between the USSR and the USA to build bigger and better weapons than the other side.

> **Investment**
>
> Spending money to improve machinery and therefore increase industrial output.

Summary Box 9

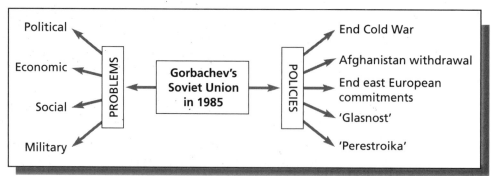

Key Topic

10 The consequences of Gorbachev's policies

What were the military consequences?

- The Soviet Union and the USA agreed to destroy many of their nuclear weapons.

- In 1989 the Red Army pulled out of Afghanistan.

What were the socio-economic consequences?

- Gorbachev's 'Law on Enterprise' gave factories the freedom to set prices and wages.
  - The result was that both prices and wages shot up, causing massive inflation.
  - Workers became less enthusiastic as higher wages simply led to higher prices.
  - Greater freedom meant that people criticised Gorbachev and demanded more.
- In 1949 **COMECON** had assured the Soviet Union very favourable trading with eastern Europe.
  - The break up of eastern Europe meant the Soviet Union no longer had a cheap supply of imports, and their export markets also disappeared.
- This meant that for the first time since the Second World War rationing was introduced into the Soviet Union.
- Gorbachev introduced a more democratic constitution that gave greater protection for the average Soviet citizen.

What were the political consequences?

- Once Gorbachev showed he would not support the communist governments of eastern Europe, the people in these countries declared their independence from the Soviet Union and moved towards democracy.
  - Between 1989 and 1991, all six major eastern European countries declared their independence from the Soviet Union.
- The Soviet Union was made up of 15 separate countries. Russia was the biggest and most powerful of these.
  - Gorbachev allowed these separate countries to begin running their own affairs, rather than Moscow telling them what to do.
  - The result was that in August 1991 these countries within the Soviet Union, such as Latvia, Estonia and Lithuania, began demanding independence.
- Unlike Stalin, Gorbachev refused to use the Red Army to force these countries to obey the authority of the Soviet Union.
- The result was that the Soviet Union split up and Gorbachev lost his authority.
- The man left with the real power in Russia was Boris Yeltsin, who succeeded Gorbachev as leader following a military coup in 1991.
- The 15 countries that once made up the Soviet Union have now loosely linked up to form the 'Commonwealth of Independent States' (CIS).

> **COMECON**
>
> A trading agreement between the Soviet Union and its communist neighbours in eastern Europe. Signed in 1949, this tied the economies of the member countries to the Soviet Union.

157

Summary Box 10

The impact of Gorbachev's policies		
MILITARY	SOCIO-ECONOMIC	POLITICAL

• 1987 – INF Treaty
• 1989 – Full withdrawal from Afghanistan
• 1989 – End of Cold War
	• 'Law on Enterprise'
	  → inflation
	  → unemployment
	  → strikes
	  → rationing
	• Collapse of COMECON
	• Soviet trade collapses
		• Collapse of Communist Bloc
		• Disintegration of the Soviet Union
		• Emergence of Boris Yeltsin
		• Disappearance of Gorbachev's role

What do I Know?

1 When did Mikhail Gorbachev come to power?
2 Whom did he succeed?
3 What had Brezhnev labelled as reasons for the country's failure?
4 What is 'glasnost'?
5 What is 'perestroika'?
6 What economic impact did the break-up of eastern Europe have on the Soviet Union?
7 Who succeeded Gorbachev as leader of Russia?
8 What does CIS stand for?

My score ………

Exam Type Questions

A typical **Section A** question:
1 How successfully had Stalin established a totalitarian dictatorship by the end of the 1930s? (7)

Answer 1

By the end of the 1930s Stalin had destroyed all of his opponents. The peasants did as they were told and workers were too frightened to slack off. Even men like Trotsky were eliminated in the purges so that Stalin was left in charge. Stalin was the only one left in charge and everyone was so scared of him they always did as they were told and everyone admired him as well.

Examiner's Comments on: Answer 1

3 out of 7

The candidate touches on the key factors but they are not explained or developed in any depth. In addition, a number of important factors have been missed out, e.g. the gulags, NKVD, show trials, propaganda, censorship, education and the Cult of Personality.

A typical **Section B** question:

2 How successful were Stalin's policies in industry and agriculture in modernising the Soviet Union? **(10)**

Answer 2

Stalin's attempts at modernisation had some successes, particularly in industrial production, but involved huge human costs.

The shift to collective farms was extremely painful for the Soviet people and not particularly productive. It aimed to feed the Soviet people but instead led to the terrible famine of 1932-3 and the policy of de-kulakisation - in total over 13.5 million people died. Between 1928 and 1932 Soviet livestock numbers fell by over 50 per cent, whilst the availability of all major foodstuffs in Soviet towns fell. Soviet grain production fell from 150 million tonnes in 1930 to just 58 million tonnes in 1935. Thereafter production gradually rose. Since then the Soviet Union has never again suffered another famine. This was made possible by the increased use of modern fertilisers and machinery, like tractors and combine harvesters.

Soviet industry was more successful. Between 1928 and 1937, coal, iron and steel production rose, and between 1932 and 1937, electricity production increased. Also new hospitals, schools, universities, metro-systems, railways, canals and dams were built. However, this progress involved a huge human cost; millions were purged and disappeared in the gulags, workers were forced to work by the NKVD or within an atmosphere of accusations like 'slackers' or 'doubters'.

Perhaps the simplest measure of success was the Soviet Union's victory in the Second World War. This victory not only proved how much the Soviet Union had progressed but also justified Stalin's methods. However, it is also possible that the Soviet Union could have made equal progress without the people having to suffer as much.

Examiner's Comments on: Answer 2

8 out of 10

This candidate has written a good response. It is well organised into clear paragraphs whilst their knowledge and understanding is detailed and clearly expressed. In addition the candidate gives balanced views about industrialisation and collectivisation, seeing their successes as clearly as their failures. Above all the candidate's personal opinion comes across strongly, especially in the conclusion.

11. Superpower relations, 1945–90

Between 1945 and 1990 relations between the Soviet Union and the USA shifted from a wartime alliance against Germany to a dangerous Cold War. The rivalry almost resulted in all out nuclear war. By the late 1960s both superpowers sought better relations and an end to their conflict. By the late 1980s, Mikhail Gorbachev and Ronald Reagan made this a real possibility. In Malta in 1989, Mikhail Gorbachev and President George Bush declared an end to the Cold War.

You will need to know why a Cold War had developed by the late 1940s and the series of incidents, such as the Cuban Missile Crisis, that almost resulted in war. In addition you will need to understand why both superpowers sought improved relations from the 1960s onwards and how this resulted in the eventual end of the Cold War.

1 Was there really a wartime alliance?

- Throughout the Second World War the Soviet Union and the USA had united to defeat the threat of Nazi Germany:
  - US posters read, 'Work like your Russian comrades'.
  - In June 1944 (D-Day) US and Allied soldiers attacked the Nazis from the west and therefore eased the pressure on the Soviet Union in the east.
  - Before 1944 the USA had given almost $11 billion worth of aid, called 'Lend Lease', to help the Soviet war effort.
  - Joseph Stalin and President Roosevelt had built up a relatively warm and trusting relationship.
- However, all was not well. Before the Second World War the two countries had become suspicious of one another. Some called their wartime alliance a 'marriage of convenience'. This means they would only be allies until Germany was beaten. There seemed plenty of evidence of this 'uneasy alliance':
  - The Soviet Union was a communist/Marxist society. Karl Marx had predicted the end of capitalist countries like the USA and urged the working classes to unite and throw off their government's control. Therefore both sides were ideologically opposed.
  - Stalin was very angry that the USA had waited until June 1944 to launch D-Day. He suspected the USA had waited until the Nazis were all but beaten by the Soviet Union.
  - 60 times more Soviet citizens were killed in the war (28 million Soviet deaths) compared to 400,000 US losses.

- Americans feared that the Soviet Union would continue invading the rest of Europe in an attempt to spread its communist beliefs.
- The Soviet Union feared that the USA would continue invading the rest of Europe in an attempt to defeat communism and replace it with capitalism and democracy.
- When the USA invented the atomic bomb, Stalin was convinced that the Americans were preparing an attack.
- When Roosevelt died in April 1945 his successor, Truman, did not get on well with Stalin. Truman upset Stalin when he compared him to Hitler!

Summary Box 1

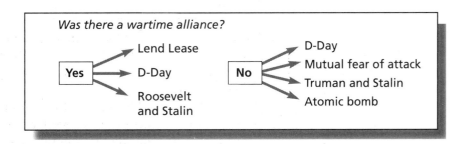

Was there a wartime alliance?

Yes → Lend Lease
Yes → D-Day
Yes → Roosevelt and Stalin

No → D-Day
No → Mutual fear of attack
No → Truman and Stalin
No → Atomic bomb

Key Topic

2 What happened at the Yalta and Potsdam conferences?

- By the beginning of 1943 the Allies felt confident that Germany would eventually be defeated. Therefore they began a series of conferences to decide what would happen after the war.
- **YALTA – February 1945**
  - Japan was to be attacked by the USSR after Germany had been defeated.
  - United Nations Organisation to be set up after the war.
  - Division of Germany and Berlin into four 'zones of occupation' after the war.
  - East European governments to have free elections after the Nazis had been defeated.
- Roosevelt and Stalin got on well at Yalta. Privately they seemed to accept the other superpower's right to dominate and control 'their half' of Europe. They called this their **'spheres of influence'**.

Sphere of influence

An area of land under the economic, military and political control of another country.

- However, several issues were not resolved at Yalta. Therefore both superpowers agreed to meet again in July–August 1945. A number of events happened in between these conferences.
  - Germany had been defeated and Hitler was dead.
  - Roosevelt had died and was replaced by Truman.
  - The Soviet Red Army now occupied the whole of eastern Europe.
  - The western Allies (USA, France, Britain) now occupied the whole of western Europe.
- The Potsdam conference did not go as well as Yalta and divisions between the Soviet Union, on one hand, and Britain and the USA on the other, were much more obvious.

- **POTSDAM – July–August 1945**
  - Japan would be attacked as planned within a few weeks.
  - Anything of value could be taken from Germany as reparations.
  - Nuremberg trials set up to deal with Nazi war criminals.
  - Eastern border of Poland would be moved west to the rivers Oder and Neisse, and all non-Poles would be sent back to Germany.
- The Potsdam Conference ended without agreement on what would happen to the newly liberated states across Europe. Both superpowers left Potsdam determined to keep their half of Europe.
- During the conference Truman deliberately hinted to Stalin that the US had successfully exploded an atomic bomb. Stalin took this as a threat from the USA. As a result Stalin became convinced that the USA would use atomic weapons if she did not get her own way.
- In 1946 Churchill made his famous 'Iron Curtain' speech, in which he said that countries in the West were free, and that countries in the East were under communist control behind an 'Iron Curtain'.

Summary Box 2

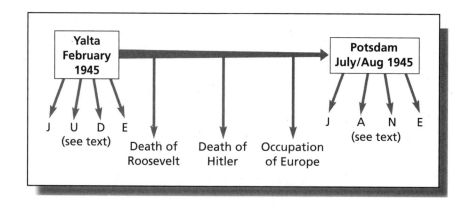

What do I Know?

1 What was the wartime alliance between the USA and the Soviet Union sometimes called?
2 Give three reasons why the Soviet Union was suspicious of the USA/western Allies.
3 Who succeeded Roosevelt as US President in April 1945?
4 When did the Yalta Conference take place?
5 What was agreed at Yalta?
6 When did the Potsdam Conference take place?
7 When did Churchill make his 'Iron Curtain' speech?

My score ....

Key Topic

3 What happened to eastern Europe after the Second World War?

- When we refer to eastern Europe we mean Poland, Hungary, Bulgaria, Romania, East Germany and Czechoslovakia. During the Second World War these countries had been occupied by the Nazis and were liberated by the Soviet Union in 1945. The Soviet Union was determined to make sure that all of these countries remained friendly with the Soviet Union after the Second World War.
- Between 1945 and 1948 elections for new governments took place in each of these countries. Stalin ordered the elections to be rigged. Pro-democracy leaders were usually imprisoned or executed.
- Therefore each country 'elected' a communist who had been approved by Stalin personally.
- These leaders were known as 'puppet leaders' and took all their key orders from Moscow.

- Stalin was determined that eastern Europe would act as a 'buffer zone', or cushion, against any future attack from the West.
- In 1949 COMECON (Council for Mutual Economic Aid) was set up. This was an economic trade agreement between all communist countries in Europe. Eastern Europe was now totally dependent on the Soviet Union.
- In 1955 the Warsaw Pact was signed to ensure that all eastern European countries (and the Soviet Union) would remain united in any war.
- It was clear to the world that the Soviet Union would not allow eastern Europe to become democratic, capitalist or allied with the West.

Summary Box 3

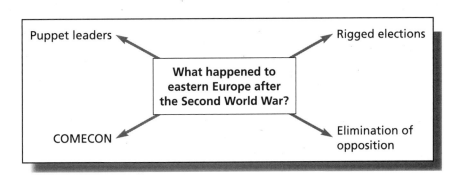

Key Topic

4 What happened to western Europe after the Second World War?

The military struggle to defeat communism

- The US government was uncertain how to respond to the Soviet takeover of eastern Europe. They knew they were unable to force them back as the Red Army was too strong.

Containment

To prevent the spread of communism.

- An advisor to Truman, George Kennan, came up with the idea of **'containment'**. He said the USA's best hope was to contain the spread of communism rather than defeat it on the battlefield. He believed the USA should now aim to stop any further spread of communism.
- This 'Containment Theory' remained US policy throughout the entire Cold War.
- Truman used this idea as the basis of the 'Truman Doctrine' in 1947. Truman said, 'I believe that it must be the policy of the United States to support free peoples who are resisting attempted subjugation by armed minorities or by outside pressures.' This meant that the USA was prepared to help any country under threat from communism.
- The Truman Doctrine provided money, arms and soldiers to defend Greece, Korea, Cuba, South Vietnam, Afghanistan and South America from communist attacks over the following years.

The economic struggle to defeat communism

- George Marshall (US Secretary of State) described western Europe in 1946 as 'ripe for communism' because of the devastation it had suffered throughout the war.
- In June 1947, rather than western European countries turning to the communist Soviet Union for economic aid, the US government sent $13 billion worth of aid to rebuild their economies. This was called Marshall Aid.
- West European economies then experienced a post-war boom. Capitalism and trade with the USA was safe.
- Marshall described Marshall Aid as a policy against 'hunger, poverty, desperation and chaos'.
- Stalin described Marshall Aid as a gimmick that tricked western Europe into an economic reliance on the US.
- By 1949, western European countries all had democratically-elected governments and strong trading links with, and an economic dependency on, the USA.

Summary Box 4

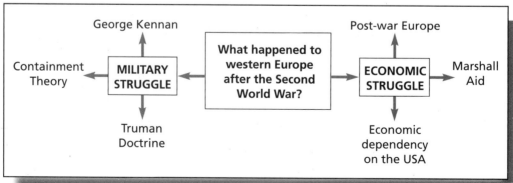

**What do
I Know?**

1 What were the leaders of the eastern European countries known as?
2 What did Stalin want to use eastern Europe as?
3 What does COMECON stand for?
4 When was the Warsaw Pact signed?
5 What did the policy of 'containment' try to achieve?
6 Which countries benefitted from aid from the Truman Doctrine?
7 What was the name given to US economic help in 1947?

My score ....

Key Topic

5 Cold War crises, 1948-62

- Between 1948 and 1962 four incidents occurred that greatly affected superpower relations:

A) The Berlin Blockade

Background
- At the Yalta Conference Stalin and Roosevelt agreed to divide Germany into four independent 'zones of occupation' until the country could be reunited. The Soviet Union, the USA, Britain and France were each given a zone to control.
- Since Berlin, the capital city, was in the Soviet zone, Berlin was split up in the same way as Germany itself.
- By 1948 the USA, Britain, and France had merged their zones together to form West Germany and West Berlin. They said they did this to make recovery easier. Stalin believed this decision was against the terms of the Yalta Agreement.
- West Berlin was therefore a small island of capitalism and democracy surrounded by communism.
- After the Second World War the USA poured millions of dollars into West Berlin to rebuild it after the war. Stalin was convinced this was a ploy to try and get East Berliners and East Germans to become envious of what capitalism might bring to them.
- Stalin was angry that the Allies were planning to introduce a new currency in West Germany and West Berlin, called the 'Deutschmark'. Stalin believed this broke agreements at Yalta and Potsdam that both superpowers would agree on any decisions about Germany.
- Stalin feared that the USA and its Allies were planning to reunite Germany against the Soviet Union's will.
- Stalin wanted to force the Allies to remove their troops from West Berlin and put a stop to any plans for the reunification of Germany.
- The USA convinced the world that Stalin was plotting to take over the whole of Germany and then perhaps the rest of Europe.

What happened?

- On 24 June 1948 Stalin ordered all road, rail and canal routes between West Berlin and West Germany to be closed and blocked. He hoped to starve the West Berliners into submission. This became known as the 'Berlin Blockade'.
- The USA was never going to let Stalin get his hands on West Berlin. General Clay, the US commander in Berlin, described the USA's view clearly when he said, 'When Berlin falls, western Germany will be next. If we withdraw our position in Berlin, Europe is threatened ... communism will run rampant (throughout the whole of Europe)'.
- The Allies feared forcing their way through the blockade in case it sparked another world war. Therefore the Allies decided to fly in all the supplies to West Berlin.
- The first flight left on 26 June 1948. By September a US aircraft was leaving with supplies every 3 minutes, containing everything needed by the people of West Berlin.
- Stalin feared shooting down Allied planes as this would show he was the aggressor.

The consequences?

- Eventually Stalin backed down and on 12 May 1949 ended the blockade. This was a huge embarrassment for the Soviet Union and a propaganda victory for the USA.
- The blockade seemed to prove to the West that the Soviet Union had plans to take over Europe. Therefore in April 1949, 12 European countries, Canada and the USA formed the 'North Atlantic Treaty Organisation' (NATO). This meant that member countries would help each other if any one of them was attacked. Stalin claimed this was a deliberate attempt to threaten the Soviet Union.
- Stalin realised that without the atom bomb the USA would always win confrontations. He ordered atomic testing within the Soviet Union to be speeded up. In September 1949 the Soviet Union exploded its first atomic bomb – the arms race had begun.
- In response to the creation of NATO, Stalin helped form eastern Europe's equivalent, '**The Warsaw Pact**', in 1955 when West Germany was permitted to join NATO.

B) The Hungarian Uprising

Background

- Between 1945 and 1956 the communist puppet leaders in Hungary removed all opposition and created a strict authoritarian government.
- Schools and cinemas were filled with Soviet propaganda and the Hungarian economy simply served the Soviet Union's needs.
- Inevitably, secret opposition groups emerged and sought to become more democratic and westernised.

The Warsaw Pact

The eight members of the Warsaw Pact were: the USSR, Romania, Hungary, Poland, Czechoslovakia, Bulgaria, Albania and East Germany.

- In February 1956 Khrushchev's secret speech, in which he criticised aspects of Stalin's rule, seemed to suggest a warming of relations with the West and an end to Stalin's strict control of eastern Europe.

What happened?
- In Hungary in October 1956 opposition groups successfully united behind the liberal ex-Prime Minister, Imre Nagy, and overthrew the communist dictatorship.
- On 4 November 1956 Khrushchev ordered Red Army tanks and soldiers into Hungary's capital, Budapest. Following bitter street fighting, the opposition leaders were all captured and a new communist puppet government was installed.
- Despite pleas via radio to the USA, the pro-democracy leaders were given no US assistance.

The consequences?
- Approximately 30,000 Hungarians died in the rebellion, including 200 rebel leaders who were executed. Imre Nagy was imprisoned and later executed.
- The Soviet response to Hungarian calls for freedom proved to the West that the Soviet Union was not prepared to let go of countries within its sphere of influence.
- This event actually may have improved relations. The USA had shown the Soviet Union that it had no desire to interfere in its sphere of influence.

C) The Berlin Wall

Background
- Berlin was divided into four zones at the Yalta Conference in February 1945.
- Up until 1961 Berliners were able to move freely about the two halves of their city (except during the Berlin Blockade of 1948–9).
- Khrushchev wanted to stop this because he believed the West was using Berlin as a base for spying and sabotage.
- The real reason Khrushchev wanted to stop this free movement about the city was that all the highly skilled or most educated people opted to work in the west of the city. Also, West Berlin had recovered very well from the war, whilst East Berlin still lay in ruins. West Berlin seemed to remind East Berliners of the achievements of capitalism and the failures of communism. 20–25,000 people left East Berlin each month between 1949 and 1961.

What happened?
- On 13 August 1961 the people of Berlin awoke to find that the Red Army had constructed a fence through the middle of the city, defended by Red Army machine-gun posts. The gap in the Iron Curtain had been closed.
- The people of Berlin were trapped in either the east or west of the city.

- Very quickly these fences were changed to concrete walls and checkpoints.
- The Berlin Wall split families for almost 30 years. At least 86 Germans died trying to cross the Berlin wall.

The consequences?
- This damaged superpower relations and added to the growing belief that an eventual military conflict was inevitable.

D) *The Cuban Missile Crisis*

Background
- In 1959 a revolutionary group led by Fidel Castro overthrew the corrupt and pro-US government in Cuba.
- Castro tried to get a trade agreement with the USA in order to feed his war-torn and poverty-stricken country. The USA refused to help because it regarded Castro as a communist.
- This made Castro turn to the Soviet Union. The Soviet Union bought Cuban sugar and cigars in return for Soviet oil, machinery and permission to build a nuclear missile site in Cuba.

What happened?
- 14 October 1962: An American U2 spy plane above Cuba spotted a nuclear site under construction.
- 16 October: President John F Kennedy set up 'ExComm' – a committee dedicated to resolving the crisis. This included his younger brother, Robert.
- 22 October 1962: Kennedy ordered the US navy to blockade Cuba with 100 warships and destroy any Soviet vessel that tried to pass through the 'quarantine line'.
- 23 October 1962: The United Nations backed the USA and ordered the Soviet Union to remove its missiles from Cuba.
- The world held its breath. Would the Soviet ships attempt to break the blockade and therefore spark an all-out nuclear war?
- 27 October: Khrushchev offered to pull out of Cuba if the USA pulled out of Turkey. Kennedy agreed to the compromise.
- 28 October: Khrushchev ordered all 'cargoes' to return to the Soviet Union. The crisis was over. Meanwhile Kennedy secretly ordered the removal of US missiles from Turkey.

The consequences
- Kennedy and the US *appeared* victorious after the Missile Crisis. Khrushchev appeared to have been the one to back down; the shame contributed to his resignation less than two years later.
- In reality it was a compromise. What the world did not know was that Kennedy had secretly agreed to pull nuclear missiles out of Turkey.
- The whole crisis had a very sobering effect on the two superpowers. Khrushchev and Kennedy now searched for 'peaceful coexistence'.

- As a symbol of this desire for better relations, a 'hotline' was installed between the White House in Washington and the Kremlin in Moscow, to provide a means of immediate contact in an international crisis.
- Many historians believe that the Cuban Missile Crisis sparked off the era of *détente* (see page 171).

Summary Box 5

Cold War crises and consequences

Berlin Blockade → NATO
Berlin Blockade → Soviet atomic bomb
Berlin Blockade → Warsaw Pact

Hungarian uprising → Maintain Soviet sphere of influence
Hungarian uprising → Represents 'peaceful coexistence'

Berlin Wall → Increased Cold War tension

Cuban Missile Crisis → Hotline installed
Cuban Missile Crisis → Origins of détente

What do I Know?

1 How many zones was Germany split into?
2 When did the Berlin Blockade start?
3 How did the Allies ensure that West Berlin still received supplies?
4 When did the Blockade end?
5 How many countries formed NATO in April 1949?
6 When was the Hungarian Uprising?
7 How did Khrushchev prevent the movement of people between East and West Berlin?
8 Who was the US leader at the time of the Cuban Missile Crisis?
9 What was the 'hotline'?

My score ....

Key Topic

6 How had superpower relations changed between 1945 and 1961?

- Between 1945 and 1961 the two superpowers had gone from being allies to being on the verge of a nuclear war.
- In March 1946, at Fulton, Missouri, Churchill described how an 'Iron Curtain' had descended through the middle of Europe.
- Between 1945 and 1948 both superpowers ensured 'their half' of Europe was firmly within their control.

- The Berlin Blockade was the first Cold War incident that almost resulted in a military conflict. It ended with both superpowers forming alliances (NATO versus the Warsaw Pact) and the start of the Arms Race.

- The Arms Race cost both superpowers enormous amounts of money. Both sides seemed to think that as long as they built even more weapons than their enemy, they would be safe in any future war.

- The Arms Race involved the design, testing and mass construction of atom bombs, hydrogen bombs, nuclear bombs, Intercontinental Ballistic Missiles (ICBMs), Medium Range Ballistic Missiles, Anti-Ballistic Missiles (ABMs), bombers, fighter planes, submarines and battleships.

- In 1961 the Soviet Union exploded a 50 megaton nuclear bomb – the biggest ever. This was equivalent to 12 million lorries of dynamite.

- By the 1980s there were enough nuclear weapons to destroy the Earth's land surface and every human being four times over.

- These arms were never directly used against either superpower throughout the Cold War.

- When Stalin died in 1953 there was a thaw in relations between the two superpowers.

- Despite the Hungarian Uprising in 1956 there appeared to be a mutual feeling of 'co-existence' between the superpowers. In other words they accepted the other superpower's right to exist as long as they did not interfere with one another.

- By 1961 the construction of the Berlin Wall had raised tensions again.

Summary Box 6

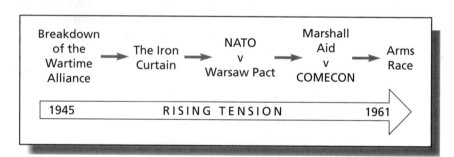

Key Topic

7 Was the era of *détente* a step forward?

Background

- By the late 1960s both superpowers wanted to improve relations with one another, for their own reasons.

- The Soviet Union feared an attack by its communist neighbour, China, and wanted an understanding with the USA if such an attack were to take place.

- The USA was fighting a very costly war against North Vietnam. A reduction in the Arms Race was needed to help limit the strains on its economy.
- Both superpowers were therefore struggling to maintain the Cold War because of political and economic problems.

The achievements of détente

- 1963: White House–Kremlin hotline set up.
- 1963: The Nuclear Test Ban Treaty banned the testing of nuclear weapons above the ground.
- 1968: The Nuclear Non-Proliferation Treaty banned the spread of nuclear secrets to other countries.
- 1969: The Strategic Arms Limitation Talks (SALT) began. The superpowers discussed ways of reducing the number of mid-range nuclear weapons.
- 1972: In May, President Nixon visited Moscow and signed the SALT 1 Treaty. This agreed to limit the construction of certain types of missiles; the Arms Race appeared to be slowing down.
- After 1972 there was an increase in trade and cultural relations between the superpowers.
- 1975: The Helsinki Agreement saw both superpowers accept the current borders of each European country and sign the Declaration on Human Rights.
- 1979: The SALT 2 Treaty agreed to limit the number of long-range nuclear missiles and extend the SALT 1 Treaty by another 5 years. This never came into effect as the US Congress refused to ratify (accept) the Treaty because:
  - On Christmas Day 1979 the Soviet Union invaded Afghanistan.
  - The invasion of Afghanistan delayed any further thawing in relations between the superpowers. However, because of the enormous economic burden of this war, the Soviet Union became even more determined to end the Cold War just six years later.

Conclusions on détente

Détente

This means a lessening of tension and better relations.

- **Détente** was not a period of friendship between the superpowers, it was simply an extended period of co-operation and agreement.
- Throughout *détente* the Arms Race continued. The race seemed to be slowing down in some areas but speeding up in others – for example, the production of shorter range, multiple warhead nuclear weapons. Throughout the early years of *détente* the Soviet Union secretly gave North Vietnam aid in its fight against the USA.

Summary Box 7

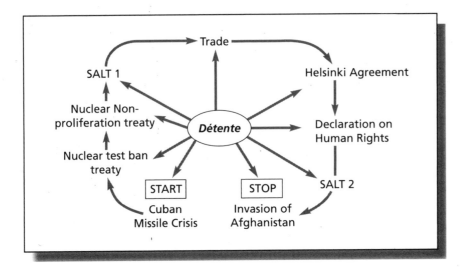

Key Topic

8 How did the Cold War end?

The war in Afghanistan

- Superpower relations got off to a bad start in the 1980s.
- The war in Afghanistan brought the Soviet Union heavy criticism from the USA, China and the rest of the world.
- The Soviet Union invaded Afghanistan because they feared that the country would be taken over by **Islamic fundamentalists** called the 'Mujahedin'.
- Brezhnev, the Soviet leader, feared that if Islamic fundamentalism were to spread any further, then the Muslim peoples of the southern Soviet Union might rise up against the Soviet Union.
- The Soviet Union believed the invasion would be brief and victorious – instead, it became their version of Vietnam.
- The **CIA** and Chinese government funded and gave arms to the Mujahedin.
- The USA even boycotted the 1980 Moscow Olympic Games in protest. (In a tit for tat move, the Soviet Union boycotted the 1984 Los Angeles Games.)
- When the Soviet Union finally pulled out of Afghanistan, 13,000 Red Army soldiers had died, along with 500,000 Afghans.
- The war placed the Soviet Union on the verge of bankruptcy. When Mikhail Gorbachev came to power he realised that the Cold War had to end if the Soviet Union were to survive.

Gorbachev and Reagan

- Both Gorbachev and Reagan faced economic problems that were forcing both superpowers to find ways of reducing their military budgets:
  - In 1986 the USA spent $367 billion on defence. As a result, the USA became the most debt-ridden country in the world.
  - Similarly the Soviet Union had run out of money. The arms race, support of countries like North Korea, Vietnam, Cuba,

Islamic fundamentalists

Extremist Muslims committed to strict Islamic laws and overthrowing foreign influence.

CIA

The USA's Central Intelligence Agency.

Afghanistan, Nicaragua, Mozambique and Angola, the space race and the enormous Red Army commitments in eastern Europe, had taken their toll on the Soviet economy.

- Despite Reagan's strong stand on communism in his earlier years, he made greater efforts than any previous president to end the Cold War. Reagan and Gorbachev struck up a strong personal friendship that suggested the Cold War would end.
- Following meetings in Geneva (1985) and Reykjavik (1986), Gorbachev and Reagan finally signed the 'Intermediate Range Nuclear Force Treaty' (INF) in 1987. This was the first time that an agreement was reached that would see the destruction of a whole range of nuclear missiles. These missiles included the Soviet SS-20 missiles and the US Cruise missiles based in Britain and Germany.
- In 1989 Reagan's successor, George Bush, met with Gorbachev on a battleship off the coast of Malta and declared an end to the Cold War.

The collapse of communism in eastern Europe

- During 1989 and 1990 the world witnessed the break up of the Soviet Union's sphere of influence in eastern Europe. All the Warsaw Pact countries threw off their communist governments and replaced them with democratically elected governments.
- The first sign that communism was collapsing in eastern Europe came in Poland in 1989. Following protests against food shortages and inflation led by Lech Walesa's Solidarity Party, the Polish communist government permitted free elections.
- To the amazement of the world, Mikhail Gorbachev stood back and refused to send in the Red Army to reinstate communist puppet governments.
- This became a signal to all the other eastern European countries to shake off their communist governments and choose their own leaders.
- Gorbachev was not like other Soviet leaders. He felt it was unacceptable to send in the Red Army and brutally destroy all opposition.
- In September 1989 Hungary opened its borders with Austria and Austria opened its borders with East Germany. **Refugees** flooded to the West.
- In November 1989, the communist governments of East Germany, Czechoslovakia and Bulgaria all resigned and the Berlin Wall was torn down.
- Not surprisingly the Soviet Union began to collapse under the weight of criticism brought about by Gorbachev's economic reforms within the Soviet Union.
- On Christmas Day 1991 Gorbachev resigned. This act was meaningless because the Soviet Union had collapsed in all but name. The 15 republics that had once formed the Soviet Union had declared their independence and elected their own governments: Boris Yeltsin, for example, led Russia.

Refugees

People fleeing war, hunger, disease or persecution.

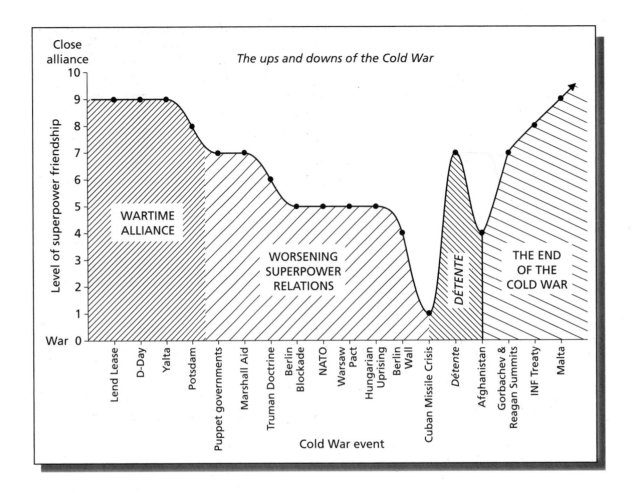

The ups and downs of the Cold War

WARTIME ALLIANCE

WORSENING SUPERPOWER RELATIONS

DÉTENTE

THE END OF THE COLD WAR

Level of superpower friendship

Close alliance

War

Cold War event

Lend Lease, D-Day, Yalta, Potsdam, Puppet governments, Marshall Aid, Truman Doctrine, Berlin Blockade, NATO, Warsaw Pact, Hungarian Uprising, Berlin Wall, Cuban Missile Crisis, Détente, Afghanistan, Gorbachev & Reagan Summits, INF Treaty, Malta

What do I Know?

1 What does *détente* mean?
2 When did the SALT talks begin?
3 What happened on Christmas Day 1979?
4 Who were the Mujahedin?
5 Who was the Soviet leader during the collapse of communism in the late 1980s?

My score ....

Exam Type Questions

A typical **Section A** question:
1 Why was there a crisis over Berlin between 1948 and 1949? (6)

Answer 1

Germany and Berlin were divided after the Second World War. In 1948 Stalin wanted to take over all of Berlin. To do this he blockaded the city and hoped to starve the West Berliners into surrendering. The USA wouldn't let the Soviet Union do this, so it kept flying in supplies. Eventually after a year Stalin gave in and West Berlin was safe again. It was a crisis because it almost led to a third world war.

Examiner's Comments on: Answer 1

3 out of 6

This candidate demonstrates sound knowledge of the Berlin Blockade and how Berlin had been split up in 1945. Unfortunately the candidate does not demonstrate an understanding of why the incident became a 'crisis'. Why did both superpowers consider the future of West Berlin to be so important that they were prepared to risk a world war over the city?

A Typical **Section B** question:

2   Why did the Cold War end in the 1980s?   **(15)**

Answer 2

By 1985 both superpowers were running up huge debts because of the Cold War. The arms race had bankrupted the Soviet economy whilst the USA spent $367 billion per year on defence. The Soviet Union had been fighting a costly war in Afghanistan that eventually cost 13 billion roubles. The Soviet Union couldn't keep up with the USA in building space rockets, submarines, warships, tanks and paying soldiers that rarely went to war. The USA looked like she could afford the arms race but was also struggling. By 1985 President Reagan was forced to borrow billions of dollars to maintain the arms race. The USA had become the most debt-ridden country in the world. Therefore in 1985 both superpowers had run out of money and were desperate to find a way of saving money – ending the Cold War was the only solution.

Fortunately, superpower relations had been improving in the 20 years leading up to 1985. The era of détente saw Strategic Arms Limitation Talks (SALT) and the signing of the SALT 1 and SALT 2 treaties. Nuclear weapons testing above ground was banned as was the passing of nuclear secrets to other countries. Despite the war in Afghanistan and the petty boycotting of one another's Olympic Games in 1980 (Moscow) and 1984 (Los Angeles), both superpowers were gradually seeking an end to their expensive and pointless conflict.

Fortunately both Gorbachev and Reagan got on very well and trusted one another. Their friendship was strong enough to break down the traditional fears each superpower had of one another; Gorbachev even became a hero amongst Americans when he made a visit in 1987. Their personal friendship led to a series of important summits and agreements. They met in 1985 in Geneva, again in Reykjavik in 1986 and finally agreed to the INF Treaty in 1987. The Intermediate Nuclear Force Treaty was the first time that both superpowers agreed to begin destroying certain types of their own missiles. Both superpowers even agreed to let the other side come in to their country and confirm that the missiles had been destroyed. After free elections were held in Poland, communism began to collapse in Eastern Europe and the Berlin Wall was destroyed. When George Bush became the President at the beginning of 1989 he met with Gorbachev on a ship off the coast of Malta. Together they declared that the Cold War was over.

Therefore through a mixture of economic problems and the warm friendship between Reagan and Gorbachev, the Cold War ended. Both sides had run out of money and run out of reasons to carry on with their conflict.

Examiner's Comments on: Answer 2

13 out of 15

Clearly this candidate has produced a good response. The answer demonstrates a detailed knowledge of key meetings and agreements in the 1970s and 80s that led to the end of the Cold War. In addition the candidate sees the causes in terms of long and short term factors, whilst appreciating the special relationship between Gorbachev and Reagan.

Practice Questions

1. Why did relations between the Soviet Union and the USA deteriorate between 1945 and 1949? **(7)**
2. To what extent did détente bring about a lasting relaxation in superpower tension? **(10)**

Mark Rowlinson

A Place to Golf

Exclusive golfing holidays
from around the world

Published in 2005 by Conran Octopus Limited
a part of Octopus Publishing Group
2–4 Heron Quays, London E14 4JP
www.conran-octopus.co.uk

British Library Cataloguing-in-Publication Data.
A catalogue record for this book is available from
the British Library.

ISBN 1 84091 455 6

Publishing Director: Lorraine Dickey
Commissioning Editor: Katey Day
Editor: Sybella Marlow
Art Director: Jonathan Christie
Designer: Victoria Burley
Illustrator: Russell Bell
Picture Research Manager: Liz Boyd
Picture Researcher: Sarah Hopper
Production Manager: Angela Couchman

Printed in China

Contents